PIZZA RULES

P I

PIZZA RULES

R U L

Peggy Paul Casella

Illustrations by Joanna Quigley-Turner

PIZZAZES

A Quick-Start Guide to Making Pizza at Home

ISBN: 979-8-218-47426-3 (Paperback)
ISBN: 979-8-218-47427-0 (E-Book)

Library of Congress Control Number: 2024919144

Illustrations by Joanna Quigley-Turner.
Cover and interior design by Danielle Deschenes.
Author photo (page 191) by Lexy Pierce.

Printed in the United States of America.

First printing edition 2025
Dough Ball Books

533 E Girard Ave
Unit #542
Philadelphia, PA 19125

www.DoughBallBooks.com
hello@peggypaulcasella.com

For

JOHN AND JACK,

the best pizza taste-testers a girl could ask for

CONTENTS

Chapter Three: SAUCES AND TOPPINGS

Chapter Four: BAKING METHODS

Chapter Five: MAKING IT A MEAL

Chapter Six: COMPOSED PIZZA RECIPES

INTRODUCTION

Until my early thirties, I didn't know making pizza from scratch was a thing regular people could do. Though my mom was a great cook, the only yeast doughs I remember her attempting were the dump-and-stir kits that came with her electric bread maker. And as I grew up and became a part of the real world, eventually stumbling into a cookbook editing career, bread- and pizza-making always seemed too scientific and time-intensive for the pace of my life. Finally, in 2013, when my then-boyfriend (now-husband) John surprised me with a 12-cup stainless-steel food processor, the stars aligned. Flipping through my shiny new appliance's spiral-bound booklet, I discovered a pizza dough recipe and figured, "why not?" (I guess, like my mother, I needed an appliance to nudge me beyond my culinary comfort zone.)

That Thursday I made my first attempt, and even though I cut corners on the rising time, rolled it out unevenly, and slathered on too much sauce, the finished product was far superior to any store-bought frozen pizza. It was perfectly browned on the bottom, crispy around the edges, and chewy under the weight of its toppings. "I could eat this every night forever," declared John.

The next Thursday I worked on my rolling and stretching techniques, and the Thursday after that I remembered to preheat my baking stone and made legit Margherita. Before long, as we tinkered with different flavor combinations and seasonal ingredients (and as I trial-and-errored my way toward the perfect pizza crust), Thursday became our favorite night of the week. A household ritual—and matching food blog—were born.

Now, more than a decade later, I've swapped out the food processor for a bowl and dough whisk, Thursday Night Pizza hosts the largest collection of unique pizza recipes on the Internet, and here I am, writing the introduction for my *second* pizza cookbook. What started as a personal cooking challenge has evolved into a passion for empowering others to make pizza at home.

HOW TO USE THIS BOOK

Pizza Rules is a fully customizable guide to the pizza-making process. Unlike other cookbooks, it's meant to spark creativity and teach you all the skills and techniques you need to bake up masterpieces (masterpizzas?) of your own.

IF YOU'RE A NEWBIE, start at the beginning and work your way from equipment and ingredients to pizza dough 101, sauces and toppings, baking methods, etc. Or, if you need more structure, try a few composed pizza recipes in chapter 6 and reference the other sections as questions arise.

IF YOU'RE A PIZZA PRO, expand your dough horizons in chapter 2, find inspiration in the mix-and-match toppings chart starting on page 88, and dabble with the various baking methods in chapter 4.

IF YOU'RE SOMEWHERE IN BETWEEN, dip in and out of the technique chapters as needed, explore the different dough and sauce recipes, and use the toppings chart (page 88) to switch up your pizza night repertoire.

REGARDLESS OF YOUR SKILL LEVEL, use the guided notebook pages at the end of each chapter to record your own dough and pizza recipes, actual rising and baking times, planning timelines, brainstorms, etc., and keep this book in your kitchen for easy reference.

7 REAL-LIFE PIZZA RULES

1. **OPEN YOUR MIND.** Repeat after me: "There's no wrong way to make pizza, and there are no wrong topping choices." Experiment with different doughs (page 34), toppings (page 88), and baking methods (page 124), and use the notebook pages at the end of each chapter to record what you like—and what you'd do differently next time.

2. **THINK "LESS IS MORE."** If you pile on too many ingredients, your dough won't bake all the way through. Make sure you can see the dough (or sauce) through the toppings, and create a balance of flavors. For example, use a light hand for strong-flavored ingredients like olives, and be more generous with mild flavors like green bell peppers. (See page 80 for suggested amounts.)

3. **GET CREATIVE.** Find inspiration in seasonal produce; special-
    ty preserved vegetables, sauces, and spreads; and small-batch
    cheeses or cured meats. Or, create pizza versions of your fa-
    vorite recipes, like moussaka, pasta all'arrabbiata, tacos, or
    Greek salad. (Flip to chapter 3 for lots of different topping
    ideas.)

4. **CRANK UP THE HEAT.** Pizza dough is meant to be cooked at very
    high temperatures. So, set your oven to at least 500°F and let
    it preheat for about 45 minutes before baking. The heat allows
    the dough to get crispy on the outside and nice and chewy on the
    inside.

5. **USE YOUR SENSES.** All the recipes in this book include proofing
    and baking/cooking times. However, the best way to know when a
    batch of dough is done proofing or a pizza is done baking is
    to use your senses of touch, smell, and sight. Dough is gener-
    ally ready to be balled up when it smells yeasty and you can
    see bubbles on the bottom, dough balls are ready to stretch when
    you poke them with your finger and they don't bounce right back,
    and pizzas are ready to take out of the oven when they're evenly
    browned across the bottom.

6. **MAKE IT A PARTY.** Ask your partner, kid(s), or guests to prep top-
    pings, stretch or roll out dough, help bake the pizzas, or add
    finishing touches like fresh herbs or drizzles of oil or hot
    honey. Involving more people in the process takes work off your
    plate—and creates opportunities for deeper connections.

7. **BREAK THE RULES.** Master a few different doughs and sauces, try
    one or two of the composed pizzas in chapter 6, then tinker
    with amounts, ingredients, and baking methods to make your own
    unique recipes.

WATCH ME IN ACTION

Scan here for 20+ exclusive
video tutorials.

Chapter One

STOCKING YOUR PIZZA KITCHEN

You don't need fancy gadgets or ingredients to make your own pizza at home—just a few basics and maybe one or two specialty tools will do the job. In this chapter, you'll learn how to set up your kitchen for pizza-making success, from must-have equipment to fun upgrades and staple ingredients.

ESSENTIAL EQUIPMENT

If you make meals in your home kitchen, it's likely that you already have most, if not all, of the tools you need to make pizza. Take a quick inventory before you dive into the recipes in this book, and gather the following items.

FOR MAKING DOUGH

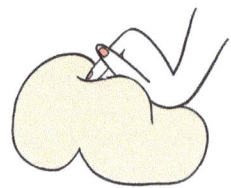

LARGE BOWL WITH A LID — Any large bowl will work just fine. However, a set of nesting stainless-steel or glass bowls with tight-fitting lids are a helpful upgrade for proofing and cold-fermenting. The main benefit of using a glass bowl is that you can watch the dough's fermentation progress without opening the lid. The main benefit of using stainless steel is that it retains heat a bit better, which aids in the fermentation of the dough, and many steel bowls come with silicone-coated bottoms, which keep them steady on the counter while you stir and knead the dough.

STURDY WOODEN SPOON — Chances are, you already have one of these in your kitchen. In your pizza exploits, you'll need it for stirring dough ingredients and sautéing veggies and other cooked toppings.

MEASURING CUPS AND SPOONS — If you want your dough to come out right every time, you'll need to use the correct amounts of dry and wet ingredients. A 2-cup liquid measure, a set of dry measuring cups, and a set of measuring spoons are all you need for the recipes in this book.

ROLLING PIN — If you're short on time and need to make pizza before the dough is finished proofing or has come to room temperature, or if you don't feel like stretching it (page 42), just roll it out. A rolling pin can help ensure an even thickness, which is especially useful when piling on heavy toppings.

QUART-SIZE AIRTIGHT CONTAINERS — Whether or not you choose to make cold-fermented pizza dough (which is balled up and refrigerated in separate sealed containers), you'll like having extra quart-size containers around for prepped-ahead toppings, extra dough balls, and leftover sauce.

FOR MAKING SAUCE AND PREPPING TOPPINGS

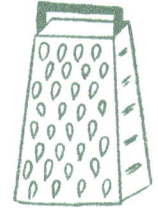

BOX GRATER — Not only will you need this for grating and shredding cheese, but you can also use the large blade side to slice potatoes and other veggies super thin.

MIXING AND PREP BOWLS — For best results (and to keep yourself from getting frazzled when the dough is ready to be topped), prep all cheeses, sauces, and other toppings ahead of time, and arrange them in separate ramekins or small bowls on your work surface. A set of four to six small and medium prep bowls and a few larger nesting bowls are very helpful, especially if you're making multiple pizzas and want to divide the toppings evenly.

CUTTING BOARDS IN VARIOUS SIZES — Use small and medium ones for prepping fresh fruits and vegetables (save one just for onions and garlic if you can, to prevent their strong flavors from leeching onto milder ingredients), and use a large one for cutting and serving your finished pizzas.

CHEF'S KNIFE — One big chopping knife is all you need for the recipes in this book. Pro tip: Keep it sharp to reduce tears when cutting onions!

BASIC POTS AND PANS — Most toppings can go on raw, but if you like bacon or sausage or caramelized onions on your pizza, for instance, you'll need something to cook them in.

BASIC COOKING UTENSILS — Whatever you have in that catch-all cookware drawer or utensil crock will suffice for the recipes in this book. The tools I use most frequently for pizza toppings are tongs, a spatula, a wooden or silicone-coated spoon, and a whisk.

FOR TOPPING, BAKING, AND SERVING THE PIZZA

LARGE SPOON — Sure, you could use a ladle for saucing pizzas, just like you've seen at your favorite pizzeria, but I find that a large spoon works just as well.

PASTRY BRUSH — For pizzas that don't have a sauce, a light coating of olive oil helps stick toppings to the dough, prevents dryness, and adds flavor. Though you could just drizzle on the oil and spread it out with your fingers or the back of a spoon, a pastry brush will give you the best results. It's also a great tool for spreading a little oil on the exposed edges of dough to get an extra-crispy, golden-brown crust.

DARK-COLORED, HEAVY-DUTY RIMMED BAKING SHEET — No, not that thin, rimless cookie sheet you use during the holidays. You'll be baking pizzas at high temperatures (500°F), so you want to make sure your baking sheet or pizza pan is thick enough that it won't warp and disrupt the toppings halfway through cooking. And yes, the color does matter. If you don't already have a dark-colored pizza pan or baking sheet, I recommend you buy one (or two); the darker metal absorbs and radiates more heat, which results in better browning and crispier pizza crust.

OVEN MITTS — Make sure you protect your hands when transferring homemade pizzas in and out of the hot oven.

PIZZA CUTTER — A sharp knife or kitchen shears will suffice in a pinch, but if you're adding pizza to your weekly meal rotation, you might as well get yourself the right tool for the job. (Learn about the different types on page 21.)

NEXT-LEVEL TOOLS AND EQUIPMENT

The following tools can make the pizza-making process a little easier—and even more fun.

FOR MAKING DOUGH

DANISH DOUGH WHISK—This tool consists of a flat metal coil attached to a wooden handle. Its loosely wound design works like the dough hook on a stand mixer, combining wet and dry ingredients with ease and cutting through thick dough without getting clogged. If you find yourself making pizza dough by hand on the regular, this is well worth the $15 investment.

KITCHEN SCALE—Some of the dough recipes in this book, such as Neapolitan (page 56), are based on exact ratios of dry ingredients to water (a.k.a. hydration) and therefore will turn out more consistently if you measure the flour by weight. To measure with a kitchen scale, place a large bowl on the scale, press the ON button, then spoon in the flour until it reaches the correct weight. A bonus of this method is that you'll have one less measuring cup to wash later!

ELECTRIC STAND MIXER WITH DOUGH HOOK ATTACHMENT OR LARGE FOOD PROCESSOR WITH DOUGH BLADE—Most of the dough recipes in this book are made using nothing but a bowl, a spoon, and your hands, but some do require a stand mixer or food processor for longer, hands-off kneading.

BENCH SCRAPER—Chopping dough into equal-size pieces and scraping hardened flour off your countertop are a cinch with this handheld multipurpose tool.

MINI ROLLING PIN—A small (3- to 4-inch), wooden rolling pin can be useful for flattening dough balls and getting an even thinness in the center of the dough while keeping the edges nice and thick.

DOUGH DOCKER — *Docking* means poking small holes in dough to prevent unwanted bubbles during baking. Though a fork works perfectly well for this purpose, a dough docker—a small roller covered with stainless steel or hard plastic spikes—will save you some time if you're making pizzas for a crowd.

FOR MAKING SAUCE AND PREPPING TOPPINGS

GARLIC PRESS — When you need minced garlic but don't want to stink up another cutting board or your hands, this tool really comes in handy. Just open the press, plop in a peeled garlic clove, and squeeze.

MORTAR AND PESTLE OR FOOD PROCESSOR — Pesto and tapenades make delicious bases for all sorts of pizza topping combinations, and they are easy to make, as long as you have a food processor or a mortar and pestle. A mortar and pestle (a bowl made of hard wood, metal, ceramic, or stone that comes with a club-shaped grinding tool) is also handy for making quick flavored oils to brush on dough or drizzle over finished pizzas (see page 82).

IMMERSION BLENDER — To make perfect crushed tomatoes, plunge an immersion blender into an open can of high-quality whole peeled tomatoes and process until they look like sauce. (See page 84.)

MANDOLINE SLICER — Cut potatoes, zucchini, and other vegetables into uniform, extra-thin slices for a pretty presentation and perfectly tender texture on pizza.

FOR TOPPING, BAKING, AND SERVING THE PIZZA

OIL STOPPER/POURER — A lot of my pizza recipes are finished with a drizzle of olive oil after baking. Instead of adding a separate oil drizzling container (a.k.a. cruet) to your arsenal of cooking equipment, simply plug this stopper into the top of your olive oil bottle and you're ready to measure oil for recipes, drizzle it onto stretched- or rolled-out dough, and give fresh-baked pizzas an extra boost of flavor.

PARCHMENT PAPER — This heat-resistant, nonstick paper is useful for lining baking sheets before roasting veggies and rolling out thin-crust (page 59), tavern-style (page 61), and gluten-free (page 64) doughs.

ROUND, DARK-COLORED PERFORATED PIZZA PAN — If you prefer to bake your pizzas in a pan, the best option is nonstick carbon steel with holes (perforations) punched into it. (The perforations prevent moisture from collecting in the bottom, allowing the crust to get nice and crispy.) In fact, this is a worthy investment even if you typically bake pizzas on a stone or steel; it's my go-to surface for reheating slices in the oven.

CAST IRON PIZZA PAN — If you want a bubbly, crispy-brown crust but don't have room (or patience) for a baking stone/steel and pizza peel, cast iron is your best bet. Go the multipurpose route with a large cast-iron skillet, or splurge on a 14-inch round iron pizza pan with handles. (See page 130 for baking instructions.)

BAKING STONE OR STEEL — When you're ready to take your pizza skills to the next level, invest in a baking stone or steel plate, which preheats with the oven to create a direct-heat, high-temperature cooking environment that's ideal for pizza. (Learn more about baking stones and steels on page 20.)

PIZZA PEEL — This is a giant metal or wooden spatula used for launching topped pizza dough onto a hot baking stone or steel in the oven. Though you could use an upside-down baking sheet instead, a pizza peel is uniquely designed for this task. Once you master the technique (see page 129 for a video demo), it's really quite easy to use.

OUTDOOR PIZZA OVEN OR GRILL — Want to replicate the charred, smoky crusts from your favorite wood-fired pizzeria? Bake pizzas in a gas or charcoal grill (see page 134 for instructions), or invest in an outdoor pizza oven (see page 132).

Continues on page 22

CARING FOR YOUR

BAKING STONE, STEEL BAKING PLATE, OR CAST-IRON PIZZA PAN

Intimidated by these heftier pizza baking surfaces? Don't be! Though they are bulky, baking stones, steel plates, and cast-iron pans/skillets only require a small amount of maintenance — and really will last forever if you treat them right.

ONE IMPORTANT NOTE: No matter how often you clean them, baking stones and steels will develop dark discolorations, especially when used often. These are normal (like the natural patina on a well-used cast-iron pan) and not indications that the surface is dirty or unsanitary. Stuck-on cheese, flour, and food residue, however, should always be scraped/cleaned off after every bake. Here are general instructions for keeping your baking surfaces in tip-top shape.

How to Clean a Baking Stone

Most importantly, let the baking stone cool completely in the oven before handling or cleaning it. Sudden changes in temperature can cause cracks. Once the stone has cooled to room temperature, remove it from the oven and scrape off any stuck-on cheese or food particles with a spatula, bench scraper, or dry, stiff-bristled nylon brush. Next, wet a cloth, wring it out until it is just damp, and wipe the stone to remove any remaining residue. For extra-stubborn, burnt-on cheese, make a paste with baking soda and a little water, rub it on, let it sit for 30 minutes to an hour, and remove it with a dry brush or towel. Let the stone air dry for an hour or two, then wipe it one more time with a dry cloth and put it back in the oven (or wherever you store it between uses).

How to Clean and Condition a Steel Baking Plate

Though steels aren't likely to crack, they are heavier than stones and retain more heat, so it's just as important to let them cool completely before cleaning. Once the steel

has cooled to room temperature, remove it from the oven and scrape off any stuck-on residue with a spatula, bench scraper, or dry, stiff-bristled nylon brush. If you don't see any other debris on the steel, wipe it with a damp cloth and let it air dry. If it still looks dirty, wash it in hot, soapy water with a stiff brush and rinse and dry completely. After every few uses, to keep it from rusting, recondition the steel: Clean it, let it dry, rub a quarter-size amount of neutral (vegetable, canola, or flaxseed) oil on each side, bake at 400°F on the middle rack of your oven for 1 hour, then turn off the oven and let the steel cool completely before using or storing.

If you see rust forming on your steel baking plate, scrub it off with fine sandpaper or steel wool, clean the steel, let it dry completely, and recondition as directed above.

How to Clean and Condition a Cast Iron Skillet or Pan

Let the pan cool completely to room temperature, then wash it in hot, soapy water with a nonabrasive sponge or scrub brush. Rinse thoroughly, wipe it dry with a dish towel, and rub the inside and outside of the pan with a few drops of neutral (vegetable, canola, or flaxseed) oil. Set aside until all the oil is absorbed, then store.

If you see rust forming on your cast iron pan, scrub it off with fine sandpaper or steel wool, wash the pan in hot, soapy water, rinse well, and let it dry completely. Then, preheat the oven to 450°F, rub a small amount of neutral oil all over the pan, and bake it upside down on the middle rack of the oven for 1 hour. Turn off the heat and let the pan cool completely in the oven before storing.

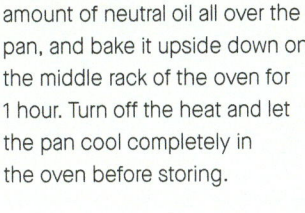

ANY WAY YOU SLICE IT

CHOOSING THE BEST PIZZA CUTTER FOR YOU

CLASSIC PIZZA CUTTER/WHEEL —
This is the most common cutter, consisting of a curved or straight handle and sharp circular blade. It's easy to use and provides great leverage for cutting all sorts of different pizzas. Just be sure to choose one with a larger (4-inch) blade if you tend to enjoy thicker-crust pizzas, and look for a bolt that can be retightened if the blade gets wobbly after lots of use.

ROLLING PIZZA CUTTER/WHEEL —
If you have little ones in the house, this option is great, since most models come with a retractable blade cover for safety. It's basically a sharp circular blade with a plastic or silicone hand grip on top, rather than a handle that extends from it. Because of this design, the rolling pizza cutter (a.k.a. pizza roller) makes it easy to cut through extra-chewy crust and hefty toppings.

MEZZALUNA (A.K.A. ROCKING) PIZZA CUTTER —
The flashiest of all pizza cutters, mezzalunas come in various shapes, some looking like elegant swords, others like jumbo bench scrapers. But no matter the shape, all mezzaluna cutters have two handles with a long, curved blade between them. Grab a handle in each hand, center the blade on the pizza, and cut through the crust in one firm, rocking motion. The only con is that the blade can get dull pretty fast.

ROUND PIZZA-CUTTING/SERVING BOARD — Once you master the art of home-made pizza, show off your skills with a pizza party! Find an extra-large wooden cutting board that can hold two pizzas at a time for an impressive family-style presentation.

SHAKER JARS FOR GRATED PARMESAN, DRIED OREGANO, DRIED CHILE FLAKES, ETC. — A selection of seasonings on the table welcomes family members and guests to make each slice their own (see page 112 for more on pizza condiments).

BASIC PIZZA INGREDIENTS

Keep these items stocked in your fridge/freezer and pantry, and you'll be able to whip up homemade pizza at a moment's notice.

Bread flour or all-purpose flour

Canned whole peeled tomatoes

Cured meats

Dried and/or fresh herbs

Extra-virgin olive oil (and flavored olive oils)

Fine sea salt

Fresh, seasonal vegetables

Freshly ground black pepper

Frozen pizza dough (see page 44)

Garlic

Hard aged cheese (parmesan, pecorino, or aged cheddar or gouda)

Instant dry yeast or active dry yeast

Jarred pizza sauce

Kosher salt

Mozzarella cheese (or any mild, semi-firm melter)

Onion

Sugar

Sketch or
write about
your dream indoor
or outdoor pizza
oven set-up.

MY FAVORITE PIZZA INGREDIENTS

Use the following notebook pages to record which brands and types of pizza ingredients you like the most, and where you found them.

FLOUR

_____

_____

_____

_____

_____

_____

YEAST

_____

_____

_____

_____

_____

DRIED HERBS AND SPICES

_____

_____

_____

_____

_____

_____

EXTRA-VIRGIN OLIVE OIL

_____

_____

_____

_____

_____

_____

FLAVORED OLIVE OIL

_____

_____

_____

_____

_____

_____

OTHER SEASONINGS

_____

_____

_____

_____

_____

_____

MY FAVORITE PIZZA INGREDIENTS

CANNED TOMATOES

_____

_____

_____

_____

_____

_____

OLIVES

_____

_____

_____

_____

_____

JARRED/PRESERVED VEGETABLE TOPPINGS

_____

_____

_____

_____

_____

_____

PREMADE PIZZA DOUGH

JARRED PIZZA SAUCE

JARRED PESTO

MY FAVORITE PIZZA INGREDIENTS

MOZZARELLA

_____

_____

_____

_____

_____

_____

OTHER CHEESES

_____

_____

_____

_____

_____

MEATS

_____

_____

_____

_____

_____

HOT HONEY AND OTHER CONDIMENTS

_____

_____

_____

_____

_____

_____

GARNISHES

_____

_____

_____

_____

_____

_____

DIPPING SAUCES FOR PIZZA CRUST

_____

_____

_____

_____

_____

_____

Chapter Two

THE DOUGH

Homemade dough might seem like the most
complicated step of from-scratch pizza, but
it's actually pretty simple. Just mix the
ingredients, knead it all together, let the
dough ferment, then ball it up and stretch
or roll it out.

In this chapter, you'll learn the basic techniques of homemade pizza dough and 10 recipes to help you recreate your favorite pizzeria menu items, from billowy Neapolitan to quick, yeast-free beer dough, slab-style Sicilian, and everything in between. Not sure which one to make? Flip to page 36 for a handy chart organized by style and fermentation/resting time.

PIZZA DOUGH 101

You don't have to make your own dough. There are plenty of delicious options at your local grocery store (bagged dough balls are always better than anything sold in a tube), and many pizzerias will sell you a ball of fresh-made dough if you call ahead. However, it does feel pretty awesome to know that the pizza you pull out of the oven is 100% made from scratch. And once you give it a try, you'll discover that making your own dough actually requires less active time and frustration than schlepping to and from the grocery store.

WHAT TYPE OF FLOUR IS BEST FOR PIZZA DOUGH?

I prefer **BREAD FLOUR** because it's easy to find and has a high (12 to 12.7 percent) protein content, which results in strong, elastic dough and crust that's crunchy on the outside and pleasantly chewy on the inside.

ALL-PURPOSE FLOUR is another popular choice, since that's the type most people keep stocked in their kitchens. It can be substituted in equal amounts in any recipe that calls for bread flour. If you use all-purpose flour in place of bread flour, you may notice that your dough doesn't rise quite as well and is more difficult to stretch; that's because this type of flour has a lower (about 10 to 11.7 percent) protein content.

TIPO 00 FLOUR is more expensive and difficult to find than bread flour and all-purpose flour, but it's known as the gold standard for making Neapolitan-style pizza dough. It is very finely ground, with a 12.5-percent protein content, and it produces a thin crust that puffs up around the edges with a delicate crunch on the outside. If you substitute 00 flour for bread flour in a recipe, you won't need all of the water; mix the dry ingredients together and stream in the water, a little at a time, until the flour has absorbed it.

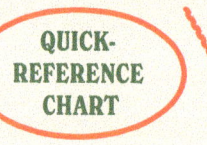

QUICK-REFERENCE CHART

PROOFING/RESTING TIMES FOR DIFFERENT PIZZA DOUGH RECIPES

DOUGH RECIPE	STYLE
1-HOUR PIZZA DOUGH (PAGE 48)	"Regular" Round-Style
NO-YEAST BEER DOUGH (PAGE 50)	"Regular" Round-Style
SOURDOUGH STARTER PIZZA DOUGH (PAGE 51)	"Regular" Round-Style
OVERNIGHT PIZZA DOUGH (PAGE 53)	"Regular" Round-Style
NEW YORK-STYLE PIZZA DOUGH (PAGE 54)	"Regular" Round-Style
NEAPOLITAN PIZZA DOUGH (PAGE 56)	"Regular" Round-Style
THIN-CRUST DOUGH (PAGE 59)	Thin and Crispy
TAVERN-STYLE THIN-CRUST METHOD (PAGE 61)	Thin and Crispy
100% WHOLE WHEAT PIZZA DOUGH (PAGE 63)	"Regular" Round-Style / Special Diet
GLUTEN-FREE PIZZA DOUGH (PAGE 64)	Special Diet
SICILIAN PAN PIZZA DOUGH (PAGE 66)	Rectangular Slab-Style

FERMENTATION TIME	RESTING TIME
1 to 2 hours at room temperature	15 minutes at room temperature
15 minutes to 2 hours at room temperature	n/a
12 to 20 hours at room temperature	1 to 3 hours at room temperature
18 to 20 hours at room temperature	30 minutes at room temperature
24 to 72 hours in the fridge	2 hours at room temperature
18 to 24 hours at room temperature, then 24 to 48 hours in the fridge	2 hours at room temperature
15 to 20 minutes at room temperature	n/a
24 to 72 hours in the fridge	8 to 24 hours in the fridge
1 hour at room temperature	20 to 30 minutes at room temperature
1 to 2 hours at room temperature	15 to 30 minutes at room temperature
1 to 2 hours at room temperature	30 minutes to 2 hours at room temperature

THE DIP-AND-LEVEL METHOD FOR MEASURING FLOUR

Most bakers insist that the only way to measure flour accurately is to spoon it into a dry measuring cup until it mounds over the rim, then level it with the flat side of a table knife. Though that method may be precise, it can be annoyingly time consuming. To get reliable results in less time, simply dip your dry measuring cup into the bag or container until it's mounded with flour, tap the rim of the cup four or five times with the flat side of a table knife, and then slide the flat side of the knife across the top of the cup to get rid of any excess flour. Using this method, 1 cup of all-purpose or bread flour equals approximately 145 grams.

GENERAL INSTRUCTIONS FOR HOMEMADE DOUGH

Intimidated by the idea of making your own pizza dough? You're not alone. Since most questions I get on ThursdayNightPizza.com are about mixing and handling pizza dough, I've written out the steps for "regular" round-style dough in extra detail*. Read this section thoroughly before you attempt your first recipe, or skim it for answers to your most burning questions.

STEP 1: MIX AND KNEAD THE DOUGH

First, mix flour with water and other ingredients to create a gluten network. Gluten is a general term for certain proteins found in wheat and other grains. When these proteins come in contact with water (or, in pizzaiolo speak, are hydrated), they bind together and form an elastic network that creates a chewy, springy texture in baked goods and traps gas bubbles during fermentation, helping yeasted breads rise. Each recipe in this chapter offers specific mixing instructions, and though a few do require a food processor or electric mixer, I generally prefer mixing dough in a large bowl with nothing but my dough whisk.

> *Want to make rectangular, slab-style (a.k.a. Sicilian) dough instead? Flip to page 66 for the full recipe and baking instructions.

Once the flour is hydrated and a shaggy dough has come together, get your hands in the bowl and squish and knead to further strengthen the gluten network, creating a strong, elastic dough that will stretch and expand as it rises in the next step.

To knead the dough by hand:

Make sure there is no more dry flour in the bottom of the mixing bowl. Turn the dough over in the bowl, then jab your fingers into it and squish the dough through your fists, moving your hands kind-of like a cat kneading with its paws. Keep turning the dough and kneading in this way until all the flour is incorporated. At this stage, the dough might be a little sticky; sprinkle in a little more flour (1 tablespoon at a time) if the dough won't stop sticking to your fingers.

NOTE: Not all of the doughs in this book require this kind of kneading. Some recipes, such as Neapolitan-style (page 56), rely instead on a longer fermentation time for optimal gluten development. Follow the directions in each recipe for the best results.

Transfer the dough to a floured countertop and coat it in the flour so it's easier to handle. Fold the dough in half, grabbing the farthest edge and pulling it up and over so the seam is closest to you. Then, press the dough down and away from you with the heels of both hands. Rotate the dough one-quarter turn, repeat the folding and pressing motion, and keep rotating, folding, and pressing for 4 to 6 minutes, until you have a smooth dough ball that springs back when you poke it gently. Make sure you don't knead much past this point; too much kneading can create too much gluten structure, which reduces the dough's ability to expand during fermentation.

STEP 2: LET IT FERMENT (A.K.A. PROOF/RISE)

This is where the magic happens. Put your dough in a bowl, cover it with a lid or plastic wrap, and set it aside for the time indicated in the recipe. The first rise (a.k.a. bulk fermentation) can take anywhere from 45 minutes (at room temperature) to multiple days (in the refrigerator). During this time, the dough undergoes a fermentation process: The yeast in the dough gobbles up the sugars in the flour and converts them into carbon dioxide, which makes the dough rise, and alcohol, which contributes to the flavor of the baked crust. Your dough is finished fermenting when it has about doubled in volume (unless otherwise stated in the recipe).

STEP 3: BALL IT UP AND GIVE IT A REST

Most of the dough recipes in this book make enough for two pizzas, so they need to be divided in half and formed into separate balls after their first rise. The purpose of balling up the dough is to strengthen the gluten network and trap carbon dioxide and alcohol inside, which will create those perfect air pockets and crust bubbles in your finished pizza.

To ball up a piece of dough:

SCAN FOR VIDEO DEMO

1. Dust the dough with flour if it feels sticky.

2. Place the dough in the palm of your hand. With the other hand, gently stretch one end underneath the dough; squeeze the seam together with the hand holding the dough.

3. Rotate the dough one-quarter turn, stretch it underneath itself, and squeeze the seam together.

4. Repeat four or five times total, until the top of your dough ball is smooth, then place it on a lightly floured work surface, seam-side down, and roll it gently with the palm of your hand.

STEP 4: ROLL OR STRETCH OUT THE DOUGH

There is no right way to prepare your pizza dough for topping—it's all about personal preference. Some people like to roll out their dough because it takes less time than stretching and ensures a perfectly even (though denser) crust. On the other hand, if you want to make pizza with an airy texture and lofty, charred crust bubbles, stretching your dough is more than worth the extra time and effort. Sure, you might tear the dough on your first couple attempts, but once you get the hang of it, you'll be surprised by how easy (and relaxing) working with dough can be.

To roll out a ball of "Regular" Round-Style Dough:

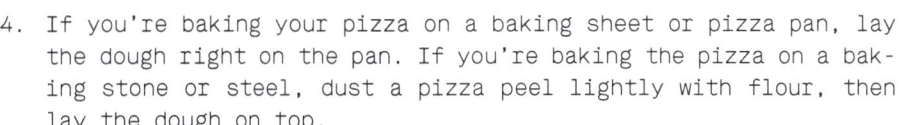

1. Place the dough on a floured work surface and sprinkle it with flour.

2. Using your fingertips, press the dough out to a flat disk about 6 inches in diameter. Dust a rolling pin with flour and roll the dough back and forth a few times to make an oval shape.

3. Rotate the dough and roll back and forth again to make a circle. Keep rotating and rolling the dough until you reach your desired pizza size and shape.

4. If you're baking your pizza on a baking sheet or pizza pan, lay the dough right on the pan. If you're baking the pizza on a baking stone or steel, dust a pizza peel lightly with flour, then lay the dough on top.

WHAT'S THE DIFFERENCE BETWEEN INSTANT AND ACTIVE DRY YEAST, AND CAN I USE THEM INTERCHANGEABLY?

Both active dry and instant (a.k.a. rapid- or quick-rise) dry yeast are granular yeasts that are used to leaven dough (cause it to rise). The main difference is that instant dry yeast granules are finer than active dry yeast granules, so they dissolve more quickly in liquid and therefore cause doughs to rise at a faster rate. I much prefer instant yeast for my pizza dough recipes, but if you only have active dry yeast, you can use that instead. Simply add another 15 to 20 minutes to the rise time of the recipe.

To stretch a ball of "Regular" Round-Style Dough:

1. Place the dough on a floured work surface and turn to coat it in flour.

2. Using your fingertips, press the dough out to a flat circle about 6 inches in diameter.

3. Pick up the circle of dough, tug gently at the edges to stretch it out a little more, then hold it like a steering wheel with your hands at the top. Rotate the dough, moving in a slow but steady rhythm and allowing gravity to stretch the dough for you. Do not rush! If the dough feels rigid and keeps shrinking back, return it to the counter, cover it with an upside-down bowl, and let it relax for 15 minutes before you try again.

4. When you've stretched the dough to an 8- to 10-inch circle, lay it over both of your fists. Start with your fists together under the center point of the dough and slowly move them apart, giving the dough a gentle stretch. Rotate the dough one-quarter turn and stretch it again with your fists, moving slowly and watching the dough to make sure it is stretching evenly. Repeat a few more times, until you have a circle about 12 to 14 inches in diameter. If you notice any thick spots in your dough, gently massage the undersides with your fist to even them out.

5. If you're baking the pizza on a baking sheet or pizza pan, lay the dough right on the pan. If you're baking your pizza on a baking stone or steel, dust a pizza peel lightly with flour, then lay the dough on top.

**SCAN FOR
VIDEO DEMO**

WHAT CAN GO WRONG WITH PIZZA DOUGH . . . AND HOW TO FIX IT

THE DOUGH IS TOO DRY OR TOO WET. If there is a lot of dry flour remaining in the bottom of your bowl when you mix the ingredients, add a little more water, 1 teaspoon at a time, just until you can work the dry flour into the dough. If the dough looks gloopy and sticks to your fingers when you poke it, work in a little more flour, 1 tablespoon at a time, or transfer the dough to a floured work surface and knead it until it no longer sticks to your hands.

THE DOUGH DOESN'T RISE. Either your yeast has expired or your kitchen's too cold. The only downside of using instant dry yeast is that you don't proof it before mixing the dough, which means that you won't know your yeast is bad until your dough doesn't rise. Always keep yeast in the refrigerator and check the expiration date before using. If you make dough within a few days or weeks of the yeast's expiration date, test the yeast before using it: Pour a little warm water into a small bowl, add a pinch of yeast, and mix until the yeast has dissolved. If the mixture foams on top within about 5 minutes, your yeast is fine to use. If nothing happens, your yeast has expired.

Another factor that can affect fermentation is room temperature. During colder months, doughs take an extra 30 minutes to an hour to expand properly in my drafty kitchen. If you have the same problem, let the dough rise in a covered bowl near (not on!) a radiator or in a warmer room.

THE DOUGH SMELLS SOUR AND ALCOHOLIC OR ACIDIC AFTER RISING. Your dough has over-fermented. During the dough's rising (or fermentation) time, yeast consumes the sugars in flour and converts them into carbon dioxide and alcohol. If the dough is left to ferment for too long, either at room temperature or in the refrigerator, the yeast will create too much alcohol, resulting in a pungent aroma that might remind you of stale beer. You can still make pizza with this dough, but it may have a slightly unpleasant flavor. Next time, watch the dough more closely as it rises, and ball it up as soon as it has doubled in volume.

F.A.Q ### CAN I FREEZE HOMEMADE PIZZA DOUGH?

Yes—it's my favorite time-saving trick! For freezing, I like to use my 1-Hour Pizza Dough recipe, since its initial rise time is short and it won't taste or smell sour/fermented after thawing out on the counter all day. However, you can freeze any dough you like, as long as it's freshly made or a store-bought dough that you can vouch for.

First, mix the dough, let it rise just until it has almost doubled in volume, then divide it into pieces and ball them up. (For most of my recipes, you will divide the dough into two balls for 12-inch pizzas or four balls for individual pizzas.) Place each ball of dough in a separate zip-top bag and press out all the air before sealing. Or, for even better results, package each ball in a separate vacuum-sealed bag.

Label the bags with the date you made the dough and freeze for up to 3 months. (Any longer than that, and freezer burn will likely affect the pizza dough's flavor.)

To defrost the dough for pizza night, simply take it out of the freezer in the morning and place it on your kitchen counter (do not remove it from its container). Let the dough defrost all day. It will gradually soften, then come to room temperature and expand a bit. If it puffs up dramatically, gently punch it down with your fist and ball it up again. Press and roll or stretch it out on a floured work surface, add toppings, and bake!

**SCAN FOR
VIDEO DEMO**

"REGULAR" ROUND-STYLE

RECTANGULAR

SLAB-STYLE

SPECIAL DIET

THIN
AND
CRISPY

Whether you're on a quest
for the perfect Neapolitan- or
Sicilian-style bake, need a quick,
no-fail recipe for weekly pizza nights,
or want to stretch your boundaries and
try something new, you're in the right
place. Flip to page 36 to choose a dough
based on style and fermentation time,
or use the icons labeled here as you
browse the following recipes.

1-HOUR PIZZA DOUGH

If you only learn one pizza dough recipe, make it this one. It takes minutes to mix the ingredients, only requires 1 to 2 hours to proof, and results in a crust that is soft and chewy on the inside, crunchy on the outside, and sturdy enough to hold any topping combo.

 MAKES 2 BALLS (ENOUGH FOR TWO 12- TO 14-INCH PIZZAS OR FOUR 6- TO 8-INCH PIZZAS)

 PREP TIME: 10 MINUTES

 RISING AND PROOFING TIME: 1 HOUR TO 2 HOURS 15 MINUTES

3 ⅓ dipped and leveled cups (483 grams) bread flour or all-purpose flour

1 (¼-ounce) packet (2¼ teaspoons) instant dry/quick-rise yeast

1 teaspoon sugar

2 teaspoons fine sea salt

1¼ cups warm (100 to 110°F) water

Extra-virgin olive oil

SCAN FOR RECIPE PHOTOS

MIX THE INGREDIENTS. In a large bowl, combine the flour, yeast, sugar, and salt. Stir with a wooden spoon or dough whisk until everything is mixed together. Pour in the warm water and stir with the wooden spoon or dough whisk until a shaggy dough forms and there is only a little bit of dry flour at the bottom of the bowl.

KNEAD UNTIL THE DOUGH COMES TOGETHER. Poke the dough with your fingertips and squish it through your fists, turning it as you go to grab every last bit of flour from the bottom of the bowl. Then, when all the dry flour is incorporated, knead the dough right in the bowl, folding and pressing the dough down with the heels of your hands, rotating it a quarter turn after each knead, until the dough no longer sticks to your hands and stays together in a smooth-ish ball. (This whole process should only take a few minutes. You could, of course, knead the dough on a floured work surface, but I prefer to save a cleaning step by using one bowl for both mixing and kneading.)

LET IT PROOF. Grease a large, clean bowl (preferably one that has a lid) with olive oil. Place the dough ball in the greased bowl and turn to coat it in the oil, then cover tightly with the lid or plastic wrap and put it in a warm place to rise for at least 45 minutes or up to 2 hours. The dough is ready to use when it has grown by at least 50 percent or doubled in volume and there are little bubbles on the bottom.

BALL IT UP AND LET IT REST. Dust a clean work surface lightly with flour. Divide the dough into two equal pieces, and form each piece into a ball by stretching the edges underneath and grabbing the bottom of the ball with your fist. Place the dough balls on your floured work surface and cover with a large upside-down bowl or a piece of plastic wrap. Let the dough balls proof for 15 minutes, until they puff up a bit. If you're only making one pizza, place the other ball of dough in a quart-size airtight container and freeze it for up to 3 months or refrigerate it for up to 2 days (thaw and/or bring it to room temperature before using).

ROLL OR STRETCH IT OUT, ADD TOPPINGS, AND BAKE. See page 58 for baking instructions.

> **VARIATION TIP:** Amp up the flavor of this easy pizza dough by adding 2 tablespoons chopped fresh herbs or up to 2 teaspoons of dried herbs to the flour mixture in step 1.

NOTES:

NO-YEAST BEER DOUGH

Who needs yeast when you have a bottle of beer in the fridge? This beer pizza dough comes together in less than 30 minutes and will wow you with its soft, chewy texture and delicious flavor. Use it for any recipe in chapter 6 that calls for "Regular" Round-Style Dough.

 MAKES 2 BALLS
(ENOUGH FOR TWO 12- TO
14-INCH PIZZAS OR THREE
6- TO 8-INCH PIZZAS)

 PREP TIME:
10 MINUTES

 PROOFING TIME:
15 MINUTES TO
2 HOURS

3 dipped and leveled cups (435 grams) bread flour, plus more as needed

1 tablespoon baking powder

¾ teaspoon fine sea salt

1 (12-ounce) bottle or can light-colored beer (such as pilsner) at room temperature

**SCAN FOR
RECIPE PHOTOS**

MIX THE INGREDIENTS. In a large bowl, stir together the flour, baking powder, and salt with a wooden spoon, whisk, or dough whisk. Pour in the beer and continue mixing until a sticky dough forms and begins to pull away from the sides of the bowl.

KNEAD UNTIL THE DOUGH COMES TOGETHER. Dust a work surface generously with flour. Scoop the dough onto your work surface, turn it until it's coated on all sides with flour, and knead it until it is smooth and elastic and no longer sticks to your hands, sprinkling with more flour as needed.

BALL IT UP AND LET IT REST. Divide the dough into two equal pieces and form each one into a ball. Cover the dough balls with a large upside-down bowl. Let rest for at least 15 minutes or up to 2 hours before using; the dough should puff up a bit, but it won't double in volume. If you're only making one pizza, place the other ball of dough in a quart-size airtight container and freeze it for up to 3 months or refrigerate it for up to 2 days (thaw and/or bring it to room temperature before using).

ROLL OR STRETCH IT OUT, ADD TOPPINGS, AND BAKE. See page 58 for baking instructions.

SOURDOUGH STARTER PIZZA DOUGH

This overnight pizza dough recipe uses sourdough starter discard and no added yeast. The result is a chewy, flavorful, airy crust that's sure to become your pizza night go-to.

MAKES 2 BALLS (ENOUGH FOR TWO 12- TO 14-INCH PIZZAS OR FOUR 6- TO 8-INCH PIZZAS)

PREP TIME: 15 MINUTES

PROOFING AND RESTING TIME: 13 TO 23 HOURS

3⅓ dipped and leveled cups (483 grams) bread flour. plus more as needed

½ cup unfed sourdough starter (a.k.a. sourdough starter discard) at room temperature

1¼ cups warm water

1½ teaspoons fine sea salt

SCAN FOR RECIPE PHOTOS

MIX THE INGREDIENTS. Measure the flour into a large bowl that has a tight-fitting lid. In a medium bowl, combine the sourdough starter, water, and salt. Mix with a dough whisk or sturdy wooden spoon until the starter is about half dissolved into the water. Dump the starter mixture into the bowl with the flour, and mix with the dough whisk or wooden spoon until most of the flour is incorporated and a shaggy dough begins to form. Take off your rings and get your hands in there, squishing the dough in your fists, turning it over, and squishing again until all of the flour is incorporated into the dough. At this point, the dough will be pretty sticky.

KNEAD IN THE REST OF THE FLOUR. Once all the flour is incorporated, dust your hands with flour and knead the dough into a smooth ball. (Press down on the dough with the heel of your hand, fold the dough up and over, turn, and repeat, dusting your hands with more flour as needed. You are done when the dough has morphed into a smooth-looking ball.)

LET IT PROOF. Cover the bowl with its lid and let it proof at room temperature for 12 to 20 hours or until it has doubled in size.

BALL IT UP AND LET IT REST. Once the dough has finished proofing, scrape it out onto an unfloured work surface. Use a bench scraper to divide the dough into two equal-size pieces, and form each piece into a ball. Place the balls in separate quart-size airtight containers

Recipe continues

(they will need space to spread out as they rise). Seal the containers and let the dough rest at room temperature until the balls have spread out and puffed up and are very pliable, 1 to 3 hours. Alternatively, seal the containers and refrigerate the dough balls for 24 to 48 hours, or place each dough ball in a separate zip-top bag and freeze for up to 3 months. (Thaw and/or bring it to room temperature before stretching and baking.)

ROLL OR STRETCH IT OUT, ADD TOPPINGS, AND BAKE. See page 58 for baking instructions.

NOTES:

_____

_____

_____

_____

_____

_____

_____

OVERNIGHT PIZZA DOUGH

This one requires a little math, but once you get the timing right, you'll see why it's my weeknight fave. Mix it around bedtime the night before, ball it up when you preheat the oven the next day, then stretch, top, and bake. The overnight ferment gives the crust a slight tangy flavor and billowy texture.

 MAKES 2 BALLS (ENOUGH FOR TWO 12- TO 14-INCH PIZZAS OR FOUR 6- TO 8-INCH PIZZAS)

 PREP TIME: 10 MINUTES

 PROOFING AND RESTING TIME: 19 TO 22 HOURS

3 ¾ dipped and leveled cups (544 grams) bread flour

¼ teaspoon instant dry/quick-rise yeast

2½ teaspoons fine sea salt

1 teaspoon sugar

1½ cups cool water

1 tablespoon extra-virgin olive oil

SCAN FOR RECIPE PHOTOS

MIX THE INGREDIENTS. In a large bowl (preferably one with a tight-fitting lid), whisk together the flour, yeast, salt, and sugar. Add the water and oil and mix with a wooden spoon or dough whisk until most of the flour is incorporated; knead with your hands just until all the flour is mixed in. The dough will be sticky.

LET IT PROOF. Cover the bowl with a lid or plastic wrap and let it rise at room temperature for 18 to 20 hours, until it has more than doubled in volume.

BALL IT UP AND LET IT REST. Scrape the dough onto a floured work surface and divide it in half. Shape each piece into a ball. If the dough feels sticky, dust it with flour. Cover the formed dough balls with an inverted bowl and let them rest for 30 minutes or up to 2 hours before using. (Or, if you're not making pizza right away, place the balls in separate zip-top bags or quart-size airtight containers and store them in the refrigerator for up to 3 days or in the freezer for up to 3 months. Bring the dough back to room temperature before stretching and topping.)

ROLL OR STRETCH IT OUT, ADD TOPPINGS, AND BAKE. See page 58 for baking instructions.

NEW YORK-STYLE PIZZA DOUGH

A true New York slice is thin yet sturdy, with a rounded outer crust that is golden brown, tender, and chewier than that of its bubbly, Neapolitan-style cousin. A touch of sugar helps the dough brown evenly in the oven, and a little olive oil contributes to both the texture and flavor of the finished crust.

 MAKES 2 BALLS
(ENOUGH FOR TWO 12- TO
14-INCH PIZZAS OR FOUR
6- TO 8-INCH PIZZAS)

 PREP TIME:
10 TO 15 MINUTES

 PROOFING TIME:
26 TO 74 HOURS

3 dipped and leveled cups (435 grams) bread flour or all-purpose flour

½ teaspoon instant dry/ quick-rise yeast

1½ teaspoons fine sea salt

1 teaspoon sugar

1¼ cups warm (110°F) water

1½ teaspoons extra-virgin olive oil

SCAN FOR RECIPE PHOTOS

TO MIX THE INGREDIENTS IN AN ELECTRIC STAND MIXER: In the bowl of an electric mixer fitted with the dough hook attachment, mix together the flour, yeast, salt, and sugar. Pour in the warm water and mix on low speed until no more dry flour remains in the bottom of the bowl, then add the olive oil and knead the dough on low speed for 5 minutes.

TO MIX THE INGREDIENTS IN A FOOD PROCESSOR: In the bowl of a food processor fitted with a metal blade or dough blade, combine the flour, yeast, salt, and sugar. Pulse a few times to mix the dry ingredients together, then pour in the water and olive oil. Process until the dough comes together into a ball that whips around the blade, then keep processing for 15 to 20 seconds.

KNEAD UNTIL THE DOUGH COMES TOGETHER. Transfer the dough to a floured work surface, turn it until it's coated with flour, and knead it a few times, dusting it with a little more flour if needed, until you have a smooth, slightly tacky ball of dough that doesn't stick to your hands.

BALL IT UP AND LET IT PROOF IN THE FRIDGE. Divide the dough into two equal-sized pieces, and shape each into a ball. Place the balls in separate quart-size airtight containers and refrigerate for at least 24 hours and up to 72 hours.

LET THE DOUGH COME TO ROOM TEMPERATURE.
Remove the dough from the refrigerator about 2 hours
before you plan to bake your pizza so it can come to room
temperature for easier stretching. If you only plan to make
one pizza, transfer the other ball of dough to the freezer; it
can be frozen for up to 3 months.

**ROLL OR STRETCH IT OUT, ADD TOPPINGS, AND
BAKE.** See page 58 for baking instructions.

TECHNIQUE TIP: If you don't have an electric mixer or food
processor, you can mix and knead this dough by
hand. Combine the ingredients in a large bowl, and
mix everything together with a sturdy wooden spoon
or dough whisk until all the flour is incorporated
in the dough. Then, scrape the dough onto a
floured countertop, dust your hands with flour, and
knead the dough for 5 to 7 minutes, until it comes
together into a smooth, elastic ball. (See kneading
instructions on page 39.)

NOTES:

NEAPOLITAN-STYLE PIZZA DOUGH

Yes, you can make restaurant-quality Neapolitan-style pizzas in your home oven, and it all starts with the perfect dough. Mix up the ingredients, let it sit at room temperature for a day, and then ball it up and refrigerate for 24 to 48 hours. The longer proof time results in a flavorful, chewy-yet-delicate crust that cooks to airy perfection in a super-hot oven (preferably on a baking stone or steel).

 MAKES 2 BALLS (ENOUGH FOR TWO 12- TO 14-INCH PIZZAS OR FOUR 6- TO 8-INCH PIZZAS)

 PREP TIME: 10 MINUTES

 PROOFING AND RESTING TIME: 44 TO 74 HOURS

3 dipped and leveled cups (435 grams) bread flour

2 teaspoons fine sea salt

¼ teaspoon instant dry/quick-rise yeast

1¼ cups cool water

SCAN FOR RECIPE PHOTOS

MIX THE INGREDIENTS. In a large bowl with an airtight lid, mix together the flour, salt, and yeast with a wooden spoon or dough whisk. Pour in the water and mix with the spoon or dough whisk until most of the dry flour in the bottom of the bowl has been absorbed by the dough.

KNEAD IN THE REST OF THE FLOUR BY HAND. Turn the dough over in the bowl, flour your hands, and squish the dough through your fists, flipping and turning the dough as you go, until no more dry flour remains.

LET IT PROOF. Cover the bowl with its lid and let the dough proof at room temperature for 18 to 24 hours (20 hours is my sweet spot) or until it has doubled in volume.

BALL IT UP AND LET IT PROOF IN THE FRIDGE. Scrape the dough onto a generously floured surface (it will be goopy with bubbles throughout). Turn the dough to coat it in the flour, then divide the dough into two equal-sized pieces and shape each piece into a ball. Place each ball in a separate quart-size airtight container. Cover and refrigerate for 24 to 48 hours.

LET THE DOUGH COME TO ROOM TEMPERATURE.
Take the dough out of the refrigerator about 2 hours before you plan to bake your pizza so it has time to come to room temperature for easier stretching. If you only plan to make one pizza, transfer the other ball of dough to the freezer; it can be frozen for up to 3 months.

ROLL OR STRETCH IT OUT, ADD TOPPINGS, AND BAKE. See page 58 for baking instructions.

> **TECHNIQUE TIP:** Since the ratio of water to dry ingredients (a.k.a. hydration) is what makes this dough so delicious, make sure you measure the flour as precisely as possible, preferably with a kitchen scale.

NOTES:
_____
_____
_____
_____
_____
_____
_____

OVEN BAKING INSTRUCTIONS FOR "REGULAR" ROUND-STYLE PIZZA DOUGH

1. Preheat the oven to 500°F (if using a baking sheet) or as high as it will go (if using a baking stone/steel); place the stone in the top third or place the steel in the bottom third of the oven before you start preheating. Let the oven preheat for at least 30 minutes. Then, if you're using a baking stone or steel, switch the oven to Broil on high.

2. Stretch or roll out your dough to a 12- to 14-inch circle and transfer it to a baking sheet/pizza pan or a lightly floured pizza peel (if using a baking stone/steel).

3. Prick all but the edges of the dough with a fork to prevent big bubbles from forming in the oven; brush the edges with a little extra-virgin olive oil if desired (this gives the crust some extra color and flavor). Add sauce, spreading it out and leaving a ½-inch border all around, then toppings. (See chapter 3 for information on topping amounts.)

4. Transfer the pizza to the oven and bake until the crust is evenly browned on the bottom and the cheese and/or toppings have browned in spots—10 to 15 minutes on a baking sheet, 6 to 8 minutes on a baking stone/steel.

5. Take the pizza out of the oven and let it sit for a minute or two, then season and/or garnish as desired; slice and serve.

See chapter 4 for other cooking/baking methods.

THIN-CRUST PIZZA DOUGH

There are a lot of great things about thin-crust pizza. You can make it from scratch in about 30 minutes; its delicate, crispy texture is great when you're craving a light meal; and it encourages a minimalist topping approach, allowing the flavor of each ingredient to shine through.

 MAKES 2 BALLS (ENOUGH FOR TWO 12- TO 14-INCH PIZZAS OR THREE 6- TO 8-INCH PIZZAS)

 PREP TIME: 10 MINUTES

 RESTING TIME: 15 TO 20 MINUTES

2 ½ dipped and leveled cups (363 grams) all-purpose flour, plus more as needed

1 (¼-ounce) packet (2¼ teaspoons) instant dry/quick-rise yeast

1 teaspoon fine sea salt

1 cup warm (110°F) water

1 tablespoon extra-virgin olive oil

Your favorite sauce, cheese, and toppings (see Topping Tip)

SCAN FOR RECIPE PHOTOS

SET UP THE OVEN. If you're using a steel plate, place it in the bottom third of the oven. If you're using a baking stone, place it in the top third of the oven. If you're using a baking sheet or pizza pan, set an oven rack in the middle position. Preheat the oven to 500°F .

MIX THE INGREDIENTS. In a large mixing bowl, whisk together the flour, yeast, and salt. Pour in the warm water and olive oil and mix with a wooden spoon or dough whisk until only a little dry flour is left in the bottom of the bowl.

KNEAD UNTIL THE DOUGH COMES TOGETHER. Flour your hands and squish the dough through your fists, flipping and turning the dough until no more dry flour remains. Then, transfer the dough to a floured work surface and knead it for about 5 minutes, folding and pressing the dough down with the heels of your hands, rotating it a quarter turn after each knead, until you have a dough ball that's smooth, stiff, slightly tacky, and springs back when you give it a gentle poke. Cover the dough with an inverted bowl and let it rest for 15 to 20 minutes.

BALL IT UP. Divide the dough into two equal-sized pieces and form each piece into a ball. If you're only making one pizza, place the other ball of dough in a quart-size airtight

Recipe continues

container; freeze it for up to 3 months or refrigerate it for up to 2 days (thaw and/or bring it to room temperature before using).

ROLL IT OUT. Work with one ball of dough at a time, keeping the other under the upside-down bowl on your countertop so it doesn't dry out. Place the dough ball on a sheet of parchment paper, then top with another sheet of parchment. Use a rolling pin to roll out the dough between the parchment to a 10- to 14-inch round, depending on the size of the dough ball and your desired thickness. The parchment prevents the dough from sticking to your rolling pin without the addition of extra flour, which can make the pizza crust too dry. If you like, you can also gently stretch the dough after you've rolled it out. Resist the urge to add extra flour unless the dough is really sticky.

ADD TOPPINGS. Peel off the top layer of parchment paper and transfer the dough (with the bottom piece of parchment under it) to your baking sheet or pizza pan. Or, if you're using a preheated baking stone or steel plate, peel off both pieces of parchment paper and transfer the dough round to a lightly floured pizza peel. Top the dough with your favorite sauce, cheese, and other toppings.

BAKE. Transfer the topped dough to the oven and bake until the crust is golden around the edges and evenly browned on the bottom, 8 to 10 minutes on a baking stone or steel, 10 to 15 minutes on a baking sheet or pizza pan. Remove from the oven, slice, and serve.

> **TOPPING TIP:** Feel free to use this dough as a base for any of the topping ideas in this book — just be modest with toppings so you don't overload your crust. For example, for a 12- to 14-inch thin-crust pizza, you'll need about ⅓ cup sauce, ½ to ¾ cup shredded cheese, and ½ to ¾ cup thinly sliced vegetables and/or meat.

CHICAGO TAVERN-STYLE THIN-CRUST METHOD

Like your pizza super-thin, but don't want to skimp on taste and toppings? Tavern (a.k.a. bar) pizza dough is cold-fermented, then rolled out and cured in the fridge overnight, resulting in a flavorful, cracker-like crust that has more heft than "regular" thin-crust pizza.

MAKES 2 CRUSTS (ENOUGH FOR TWO 12-INCH PIZZAS)

PREP TIME:
10 TO 15 MINUTES

PROOFING AND CURING TIME:
34 TO 82 HOURS

1 recipe New York–Style Pizza Dough (page 54)

Your favorite sauce, cheese, and toppings (see Topping Tip)

SCAN FOR VIDEO DEMO

MAKE THE DOUGH. Mix and knead the dough according to the directions on page 54, divide it into two pieces, ball them up, and let them ferment in separate quart-size airtight containers in the refrigerator for 24 to 72 hours.

ROLL IT OUT AND LET IT CURE. The day before you want to bake the pizza, take the dough out of the refrigerator and let it rest, covered, for 1 to 2 hours. Then, place each ball between sheets of parchment paper and roll them out to thin, even 12- to 13-inch rounds. Peel off the top pieces of parchment and prick the dough rounds all over on both sides with a fork (or dough docker, if you have one). Put each dough round with its bottom sheet of parchment on a separate platter or pizza pan; refrigerate, uncovered and unstacked, for 8 to 24 hours. The dough should look dry on top. (If you are only making one pizza, freeze the extra one now — see Make-Ahead Tip.)

SET UP THE OVEN. Place your baking stone or steel (if using) on an oven rack in the middle position and preheat to 500°F for at least 45 minutes.

TOP AND BAKE. Peel off the parchment paper and place the cured pizza dough round on a pizza pan or peel (it should be dry enough to move around on the peel when you

Recipe continues

shake it gently back and forth; if not, flip the dough so the drier side is on the bottom). Spread sauce all the way to the edges of the dough, add other toppings and cheese, and bake until the underside of the crust is evenly browned, 8 to 10 minutes on a baking stone or steel, 13 to 15 minutes on
a baking sheet or pizza pan.

SLICE AND SERVE. Remove the pizza from the oven, cut into squares, and serve.

MAKE-AHEAD TIP: Wrap the rolled-out, refrigerated (a.k.a. cured) dough in parchment paper, then vacuum seal or wrap tightly in foil or plastic wrap and freeze for up to 3 months. Take the frozen dough out of the freezer an hour or two before you want to bake the pizza, and let it thaw on the counter before topping.

TOPPING TIP: For each pizza, you'll need ½ cup sauce, 1½ cups shredded cheese, and 1 to 1½ cups of cooked or cured meats and/or sliced veggies.

NOTES:

100% WHOLE WHEAT PIZZA DOUGH

This recipe is the real deal. It contains zero white flour, very little salt, honey instead of sugar, just a touch of oil—and makes a pizza crust that's equally nutritious *and* flavorful.

 MAKES 2 BALLS (ENOUGH FOR TWO 12- TO 14-INCH PIZZAS OR FOUR 6- TO 8-INCH PIZZAS)

 PREP TIME: 10 TO 15 MINUTES

 PROOFING AND RESTING TIME: 1½ TO 2 HOURS

1½ cups warm (110°F) water

1 (¼-ounce) packet (2¼ teaspoons) instant dry/quick-rise yeast

2 tablespoons honey

3½ dipped and leveled cups (525 grams) whole wheat flour (white whole wheat or regular whole wheat), plus more for kneading the dough

2 teaspoons fine sea salt

1 tablespoon extra-virgin olive oil

Nonstick cooking spray or olive oil, for greasing the bowl

SCAN FOR RECIPE PHOTOS

MIX THE INGREDIENTS. In a large mixing bowl, whisk together the warm water, yeast, and honey until the yeast is fully dissolved. Add the flour, salt, and olive oil and mix with a wooden spoon or dough whisk until the dough comes together.

KNEAD THE DOUGH. Sprinkle some whole wheat flour on a clean counter or large cutting board. Scrape the dough onto the floured surface and knead it for about 5 minutes, until the dough ball is smooth and slowly bounces back when you poke it with your finger.

LET IT PROOF. Coat the inside of a large, lidded bowl with cooking spray, or drizzle it with olive oil. Place the dough in the bowl and turn to coat it in the oil. Cover the bowl with the lid (or plastic wrap) and let the dough rise in a warm place for 1 hour or until it has doubled in volume and you can see little bubbles on the top.

BALL IT UP AND LET IT REST. Dust your workspace with whole wheat flour. Take the dough out of the bowl, divide it into two pieces, shape them into balls, and place them on a lightly floured counter or board. (Or, place each ball in its own zip-top bag and freeze for up to 3 months.) Cover the dough with an upside-down bowl (I use the same one the dough rose in). Let the dough balls rest until they puff up a bit, 20 to 30 minutes.

ROLL OR STRETCH IT OUT, ADD TOPPINGS, AND BAKE. Roll out or stretch, top, and bake according to the directions for "Regular" Round-Style Dough, page 58.

GLUTEN-FREE PIZZA DOUGH

This gluten-free dough is made with easy-to-find ingredients, and it results in a flavorful, slightly chewy crust that's a great base for any combination of toppings.

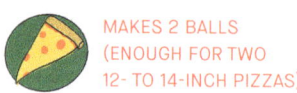 MAKES 2 BALLS (ENOUGH FOR TWO 12- TO 14-INCH PIZZAS)

 PREP TIME: 10 TO 15 MINUTES

 PROOFING AND RESTING TIME: 1½ TO 2½ HOURS

4 dipped and leveled cups (600 grams) 1-to-1 gluten-free baking flour (Make sure the flour contains xanthan gum; I had the best results with Bob's Red Mill brand)

1 (¼-ounce) packet (2¼ teaspoons) instant dry/quick-rise yeast

2 teaspoons baking powder

1 teaspoon baking soda

2 teaspoons fine sea salt

1 teaspoon dried Italian herb blend (optional)

2 cups warm (110°F) water

3 tablespoons extra-virgin olive oil, plus more for greasing the bowl

1 tablespoon honey or maple syrup

Your favorite sauce, cheese, and toppings (see Topping Tip)

MIX THE INGREDIENTS. In a large bowl, mix together the flour, yeast, baking powder, baking soda, salt, and dried herb blend (if using). Pour in the warm water, olive oil, and honey, and mix with a wooden spoon or dough whisk until a uniform dough forms, about 5 minutes (the texture will remind you of cookie dough). If your dough seems too sticky or loose, add more flour, a little at a time, until you can form it into a soft ball.

SET ASIDE TO PROOF. Grease a clean bowl with olive oil. Pat the dough into a ball, place it in the greased bowl, and turn the dough to coat it in the oil. Cover the bowl with a lid or plastic wrap and let the dough rest in a warm place for 1 to 2 hours, until it puffs up considerably (it won't quite double in volume).

BALL IT UP AND LET IT REST. Transfer the dough to a lightly floured work surface. Divide the dough into two equal-size pieces and shape them into balls. Cover the balls with an inverted bowl and let them rest for 15 to 30 minutes, until they expand a bit. If you're only making one pizza, place the other ball of dough in a quart-size airtight container and freeze for up to 3 months or refrigerate for up to 3 days.

SET UP THE OVEN. Place your baking stone or steel (if using) on a rack in the middle position and preheat the oven to 450°F.

ROLL IT OUT. Place one ball of dough on a piece of parchment paper that's a few inches larger than the pizza dimensions you're going for. Press or roll out the dough to a 12- to 14-inch circle, making sure it's as even as possible. If you like, form a mounded crust around the edges.

PARBAKE THE DOUGH. Use the parchment to slide the dough onto a pizza peel (if using a baking stone or steel) or baking sheet. Transfer to the oven and bake the dough for 5 to 7 minutes, until it looks dry and begins to turn golden around the edges.

TOP AND BAKE THE PIZZA. Remove the crust from the oven. Add your desired sauce, cheese, and toppings, brush the exposed dough with olive oil, then return the crust to the oven and bake for 10 to 15 more minutes, until the crust is golden and the toppings are browned in spots. Remove the pizza from the oven. Slice and serve.

> **TOPPING TIP:** Feel free to use this dough as a base for any of the topping ideas in chapter 3 — just don't overload it. For a 12- to 14-inch gluten-free pizza, you'll need about ⅓ cup sauce, ½ to ¾ cup shredded cheese, and ½ to ¾ cup thinly sliced vegetables and/or meat.

SCAN FOR RECIPE PHOTOS

NOTES:

SICILIAN PAN PIZZA DOUGH

If a thick, bready square of grandma- or Detroit-style pizza or tomato pie is your idea of perfection, then this is the pizza dough you're looking for. It bakes up tender, light, and airy, with a golden-brown crust that delivers just the right amount of crispiness on the bottom and edges.

 MAKES 1 (13-BY-18-INCH) SHEET PAN PIZZA OR 2 (9-BY-13-INCH) DETROIT-STYLE PIZZAS

 PREP TIME: 10 MINUTES

 RISING AND PROOFING TIME: 1 HOUR 40 MINUTES OR UP TO 26 HOURS

4 dipped and leveled cups (580 grams) bread flour or all-purpose flour

2 teaspoons fine sea salt

1 teaspoon sugar

1 teaspoon instant dry/quick-rise yeast

1⅔ cups warm (110°F) water

5 tablespoons extra-virgin olive oil, divided

SCAN FOR RECIPE PHOTOS

TO MAKE THE DOUGH BY HAND: In a large bowl, whisk together the flour, salt, sugar, and yeast. Pour in the warm water and 2 tablespoons of olive oil, then mix with a wooden spoon or dough whisk until no more dry flour remains in the bottom of the bowl. Scrape the dough onto a floured work surface. Knead the dough, sprinkling it with a little more flour as needed, until it comes together in a smooth, soft ball that is tacky but doesn't stick to your hands, about 5 minutes.

TO MAKE THE DOUGH IN AN ELECTRIC STAND MIXER: In the bowl of an electric mixer fitted with the dough hook, whisk together the flour, salt, sugar, and yeast. Add the water and 2 tablespoons of olive oil and mix with the dough hook on low speed until all the flour has been absorbed. Increase the speed to medium and mix for 6 minutes, until the dough is stretchy and smooth. If the dough sticks to your hands when you touch it, dust it with a little flour and form it into a loose, soft ball.

TO MAKE THE DOUGH IN A FOOD PROCESSOR: In the bowl of a food processor fitted with the metal blade or dough blade, combine the flour, salt, sugar, yeast, water, and 2 tablespoons of olive oil. Process until the dough comes together into a ball that whips around the blade, then keep processing for 30 seconds. If the dough sticks to your hands when you touch it, dust it with a little flour and form it into a loose, soft ball.

LET IT RISE. Grease a large bowl (preferably one that has a lid) with 1 tablespoon of olive oil. Place the dough in the greased bowl, turn to coat it in the oil, then cover the bowl with the lid or plastic wrap and let the dough rise until doubled, 1 to 2 hours at room temperature or 4 to 24 hours in the refrigerator. (If refrigerating the dough, let it come to room temperature before proceeding to the next step.)

DIVIDE THE DOUGH (IF NECESSARY). For a large baking sheet–size grandma-style pizza, keep the dough in one piece. For Detroit-style or smaller pan pizzas, divide the dough into two equal-sized pieces. (If you don't plan to make two smaller pizzas, place the extra dough ball in a zip-top bag; refrigerate for up to 2 days or freeze for up to 3 months.)

PRESS THE DOUGH INTO THE PAN AND LET IT PROOF. Grease a 13-by-18-inch rimmed baking sheet (or two 9-by-13-inch baking pans, for Detroit-style pizza) with 2 tablespoons of olive oil. Place the dough in the pan and gently press it out with your fingertips until it reaches all the way to the edges. If it keeps shrinking back, let the dough rest for another 15 to 20 minutes and try again. Cover the pan with plastic wrap or a clean kitchen towel and let the dough rest and puff up for 20 minutes or up to 2 hours, depending on the specific recipe.

ADD TOPPINGS AND BAKE. See page 176 for Detroit-style topping and baking instructions; see page 174 for grandma-style topping and baking instructions; see page 178 for tomato pie topping and baking instructions.

> **VARIATION TIP:** This dough can also be used to make focaccia. Follow the directions for Tomato Pie (page 178), omitting the sauce and cheese. Instead, once the dough has puffed up in the baking sheet, dimple it all over with your fingertips, then spread about 2 tablespoons of garlic-flavored olive oil evenly on top and sprinkle generously with dried rosemary, dried thyme, kosher salt, and freshly ground black pepper. Bake according to the Tomato Pie directions.

 WHAT'S THE DIFFERENCE BETWEEN GRANDMA- AND DETROIT-STYLE PIZZA?

Though they are similar, there are a few key characteristics that set these square-slice styles apart:

THICKNESS—After pressing it out in the pan, the dough for Detroit-style is left to rest for 40 minutes to 1 hour, which results in a thicker finished crust than grandma-style, which only rests for 20 to 30 minutes.

SIZE—Grandma-style is made in a large, 13-by-18-inch rimmed baking sheet, and Detroit-style pizza is made in a 9-by-13-inch metal baking pan.

TOPPINGS—Detroit-style has a specific order of toppings: cheese (mounded around the edge to make a caramelized "frico" crown), other toppings, and stripes of sauce on top; grandma-style can have any toppings you like, usually with the sauce on bottom.

PLAN-AHEAD SCHEDULES   FOR HOMEMADE PIZZA DOUGH

Working backward from when you want to serve the pizza, use the following charts to create planning schedules for different pizza dough recipes.

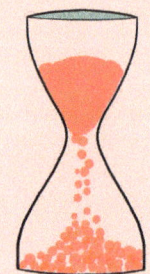

TARGET PIZZA NIGHT DINNERTIME: _____

DOUGH RECIPE: _____ (PAGE _____)

DATE/TIME	STEP	NOTES
	Mix the ingredients	
	Start first proof	
	Start second proof (if applicable)	
	Preheat the oven/ start final rest time	
	Stretch or roll out the dough	
	Top and bake	

TARGET PIZZA NIGHT DINNERTIME: _____

DOUGH RECIPE: _____ (PAGE _____)

DATE/TIME	STEP	NOTES
	Mix the ingredients	
	Start first proof	
	Start second proof (if applicable)	
	Preheat the oven/ start final rest time	
	Stretch or roll out the dough	
	Top and bake	

TARGET PIZZA NIGHT DINNERTIME: _____

DOUGH RECIPE: _____ (PAGE _____)

DATE/TIME	STEP	NOTES
	Mix the ingredients	
	Start first proof	
	Start second proof (if applicable)	
	Preheat the oven/ start final rest time	
	Stretch or roll out the dough	
	Top and bake	

TARGET PIZZA NIGHT DINNERTIME: _____

DOUGH RECIPE: _____ (PAGE _____)

DATE/TIME	STEP	NOTES
	Mix the ingredients	
	Start first proof	
	Start second proof (if applicable)	
	Preheat the oven/ start final rest time	
	Stretch or roll out the dough	
	Top and bake	

TARGET PIZZA NIGHT DINNERTIME: _____

DOUGH RECIPE: _____ (PAGE _____)

DATE/TIME	STEP	NOTES
	Mix the ingredients	
	Start first proof	
	Start second proof (if applicable)	
	Preheat the oven/ start final rest time	
	Stretch or roll out the dough	
	Top and bake	

TARGET PIZZA NIGHT DINNERTIME: _____

DOUGH RECIPE: _____ (PAGE _____)

DATE/TIME	STEP	NOTES
	Mix the ingredients	
	Start first proof	
	Start second proof (if applicable)	
	Preheat the oven/ start final rest time	
	Stretch or roll out the dough	
	Top and bake	

DOUGH-MAKING LOG

Yeasted doughs are often affected by the level of humidity, time of year, and/or kitchen temperature. Use this space to record how long it really took for your dough to double in volume and puff up during the resting step, then refer to this chart the next time you make the same recipe.

DOUGH RECIPE	DATE MADE	ACTUAL PROOF TIME	ACTUAL REST TIME	NOTES

MY SIGNATURE PIZZA DOUGH RECIPES

Once you've mastered my pizza dough recipes, hopefully taking notes along the way, why not make your own?

RECIPE TITLE: _____

YIELD: _____

PREP TIME: _____ PROOFING AND RESTING TIME: _____

INGREDIENTS: DIRECTIONS:

NOTES:

RECIPE TITLE: _____

YIELD: _____

PREP TIME: _____ PROOFING AND RESTING TIME: _____

INGREDIENTS:

DIRECTIONS:

NOTES:

RECIPE TITLE: _____

YIELD: _____

PREP TIME: _____ PROOFING AND RESTING TIME: _____

INGREDIENTS: DIRECTIONS:

NOTES:

RECIPE TITLE: _____

YIELD: _____

PREP TIME: _____ PROOFING AND RESTING TIME: _____

INGREDIENTS: DIRECTIONS:

NOTES:

Chapter Three

SAUCES AND TOPPINGS

Now that you've decked out your kitchen and made your own dough (or grabbed a high-quality premade ball from the store), it's time to talk toppings. In this chapter, you'll find six go-to sauce recipes, plus charts of pizza-friendly cheeses, produce, and proteins—complete with prepping instructions and complementary flavors to help you mix and match. Take the minimal approach with nothing but sauce and cheese, keep it classic with your favorite pizzeria order, or pick an unexpected pairing. Then, flip to page 116 to list your favorite combinations, brainstorm new ideas, and record your own recipes.

There are no perfect equations for topping a pizza, since so much depends on the size, the dough you are using, and how you plan to bake it. However, after a decade of tinkering, I've found these general guidelines pretty reliable.

TOPPING	AMOUNT NEEDED FOR 12- TO 14-INCH PIZZA
SAUCE	⅓ to ½ cup
CHEESE	4 to 6 ounces, shredded, cubed, or crumbled (1 level to heaping cup)
SAUSAGE OR OTHER COOKED MEAT	4 to 8 ounces (1 cup cooked and crumbled)
PEPPERONI OR OTHER SLICED CURED MEAT	4 to 8 ounces (½ to 1 cup)
SLICED OR CHOPPED OLIVES, SUN-DRIED TOMATOES, MARINATED ARTICHOKES, OR ROASTED RED PEPPERS	¼ to ½ cup (less if they taste salty and you're planning to use other salty ingredients like aged cheese or charcuterie)
SLICED COOKED OR RAW VEGETABLES	1 cup (or up to 2 cups if they are your only toppings)
CHOPPED FRESH HERBS	1 to 3 tablespoons, added as garnish after baking

SAUCES

It's the toppings that everyone talks about—symmetrically arranged slices of pepperoni, a confetti-like scattering of multicolored bell peppers, red onions, and black and green olives—but it's the sauce that adheres those toppings to the crust and brings it all together.

In this section, you'll find recipes for six classic green, red, and white pizza sauces that go with just about any toppings you can think of (and are also delicious on their own):

- Garlicky Herb Oil (page 82)
- Any-Herb Pesto (page 83)
- No-Cook Marinara Sauce (page 84)
- Slow-Simmered Pizza Sauce (page 85)
- Ricotta Cream Sauce (page 86)
- Deconstructed Cream "Sauce" (page 87)

WHAT TO LOOK FOR IN STORE-BOUGHT PIZZA SAUCE

Want to buy a jar instead? There's nothing wrong with that! In fact, I always keep a couple cans or jars in my pantry for those nights when I can't be bothered. Look for premade sauces that have short ingredient lists containing only foods and seasonings you recognize. For example, red pizza sauces should only contain tomatoes, oil, garlic, salt, and herbs/spices, and pesto should only contain herbs, garlic, oil, cheese, nuts, and salt.

**SCAN FOR
MORE PIZZA SAUCE
RECIPES**

MORTAR AND PESTLE GARLICKY HERB OIL

This is my fresh, herbaceous version of the garlic oil many pizzerias use as a base for classic white pies. (Just leave out the herbs to keep it "plain.") It also happens to be a great way to use up herb sprigs left over from other recipes, and it's a delicious reason to drag out that heavy mortar and pestle you wish you used more often.

MAKES ABOUT ¼ CUP
(ENOUGH FOR ONE 12- TO
14-INCH PIZZA)

PREP TIME:
5 MINUTES

2 packed tablespoons fresh herb leaves

1 medium garlic clove, quartered or roughly chopped

Kosher salt

Freshly ground black pepper

3 tablespoons extra-virgin olive oil

Put the herbs and garlic in a mortar and add a big pinch of salt and a few grinds of black pepper. Grind with the mortar until the herbs begin to break down into smaller pieces, then pour in the olive oil and keep grinding until the mixture looks like a loose pesto. Taste and add more salt and pepper as desired.

Spread it on stretched- or rolled-out pizza dough, add toppings, and bake, or drizzle a tablespoon or two over baked pizzas once they come out of the oven.

> **PIZZA PAIRINGS:** Fresh mozzarella, goat cheese, and feta are great cheese match-ups for this sauce, since they don't exude extra oil as they melt. Or, brush the dough with the herb oil, bake, then add torn burrata when it comes out of the oven. Choose vegetable and/or protein toppings that complement the fresh herbs you used for the recipe, but keep it simple so the flavors in the oil can really shine. (My favorite combo is basil-garlic oil with chopped ripe tomatoes, fresh mozzarella, and a garnish of basil or mint leaves.)

ANY-HERB PESTO

Everyone should have a versatile pesto recipe in their back pocket. This one is fully customizable and comes together quickly in a food processor. Experiment with different nuts and fresh herbs depending on the season or your desired toppings—and make sure to record your favorite combinations on page 118!

 MAKES ABOUT 2 CUPS (ENOUGH FOR ONE SHEET PAN PIZZA OR TWO TO THREE 12- TO 14-INCH PIZZAS)

 PREP TIME: 10 MINUTES

½ cup pine nuts, pistachios, chopped almonds, or walnut pieces, lightly toasted

6 packed cups roughly chopped mixed fresh herbs or greens (like basil, mint, parsley, chives, arugula, spinach, or kale)

2 large garlic cloves, peeled and halved

1 cup finely shredded parmesan or other hard, aged cheese

½ teaspoon fine sea salt

1 tablespoon freshly squeezed lemon juice

½ cup extra-virgin olive oil

Combine the toasted nuts, herbs, garlic, cheese, salt, and lemon juice in a food processor. Pulse until everything is combined and finely chopped, then add the oil and grind on low or medium speed until smooth.

Spread it on stretched- or rolled-out pizza dough, add toppings, and bake. Store extra pesto in an airtight container in the refrigerator for up to 1 week or in the freezer for up to 6 months.

PIZZA PAIRINGS: Fresh mozzarella, feta, and goat cheese are the best cheeses for pesto pizza, since they don't get oily as they melt. Choose raw veggies that taste great with garlic and herbs, such as tomatoes, peppers (sweet and hot), mushrooms, zucchini, asparagus, and green beans, or more luxurious, cooked options like caramelized onions or roasted butternut squash. For protein, try Italian cured meats, cooked shredded chicken, canned beans, or crumbled tofu.

NO-COOK MARINARA SAUCE

What's not to love about a pizza sauce that comes together in five minutes, costs just a few dollars, and tastes way fresher than any bottled version at the grocery store? Make it plain, or brighten it up with a mix of dried or chopped fresh herbs.

 MAKES 2½ TO 3 CUPS
(PLENTY FOR FOUR 12- TO
14-INCH PIZZAS)

 PREP TIME:
5 MINUTES

1 (28-ounce) can high-quality whole peeled tomatoes

1 medium to large garlic clove, minced or pressed

¾ teaspoon fine sea salt

Freshly ground black pepper

1 teaspoon dried herbs or 1 tablespoon chopped fresh herbs (optional)

1 tablespoon extra-virgin olive oil

BY-HAND METHOD: Pour the tomatoes into a medium bowl, put the bowl in the bottom of your kitchen sink to contain splatters, and squish with your hands hands or a potato masher until the tomatoes are the consistency of a slightly chunky sauce. Add the garlic, salt, a few grinds of black pepper, the herbs (if using), and the olive oil. Whisk until all the oil is incorporated.

IMMERSION BLENDER METHOD: Pour out the top inch or so of liquid from the can of tomatoes. Add the garlic, salt, a few grinds of black pepper, herbs (if using), and olive oil to the can, then use your immersion blender to process the mixture until it's as chunky as smooth as you like it. If necessary, use a fork to whisk in any pools of oil you see around the inside edges of the can.

Use immediately or let marinate for 15 minutes before using. Spread it on stretched- or rolled-out pizza dough, add toppings, and bake. Transfer extra sauce to an airtight container; refrigerate for up to 5 days or freeze for up to 6 months.

PIZZA PAIRINGS: Just about anything goes well with this vibrant, fresh-tasting tomato sauce. Start with the classics — fresh or low-moisture mozzarella, parmesan, peppers, mushrooms, olives, and Italian cured meats — then experiment with your favorite cheeses, fresh or cooked vegetables, and proteins.

SLOW-SIMMERED PIZZA SAUCE

When you want a sauce that's thick and robust and a little sweet, just like the one at your favorite New York–style pizza joint, this is your best bet. Instead of white sugar, balsamic vinegar gives the sauce its characteristic sweetness and intensifies the tomato flavor.

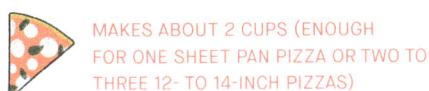 MAKES ABOUT 2 CUPS (ENOUGH FOR ONE SHEET PAN PIZZA OR TWO TO THREE 12- TO 14-INCH PIZZAS)

 PREP TIME: 10 MINUTES

 COOK TIME: 2 HOURS

2 tablespoons extra-virgin olive oil

½ small yellow (sweet) onion, minced

1 (28-ounce) can whole peeled tomatoes, crushed by hand

1 tablespoon balsamic vinegar

1 teaspoon dried oregano (optional)

Pinch of dried chile flakes (optional)

Kosher salt

Freshly ground black pepper

Heat the oil in a medium saucepan over medium-high heat and sauté the onion until it is very soft and translucent, 5 to 7 minutes. Stir in the tomatoes and vinegar and season with the oregano (if using), dried chile flakes (if using), a big pinch of salt, and a few grinds of black pepper. Bring the mixture to a bubble, then reduce the heat to medium-low. Simmer the sauce, uncovered, for 1 to 2 hours, until it has reached your desired consistency.

Remove the pan from the heat. Let the sauce cool to room temperature, then spread it on stretched- or rolled-out pizza dough, add toppings, and bake. Transfer extra sauce to an airtight container; refrigerate for up to 5 days or freeze for up to 6 months.

PIZZA PAIRINGS: This tomato sauce is thicker and sweeter than No-Cook Marinara, making it an especially great base for olives, salty meats, and cooked veggies. It's also my favorite sauce for Grandma-Style Pizza (page 174) and Tomato Pie (page 178).

RICOTTA CREAM SAUCE

Put away your saucepan and wooden spoon. The creamiest, most flavorful white pizza sauce requires zero time at the stove—just some quality ingredients, a bowl, and a whisk.

MAKES ABOUT 2 CUPS
(ENOUGH FOR TWO TO THREE
12- TO 14-INCH PIZZAS)

PREP TIME:
5 MINUTES

1½ cups whole-milk ricotta cheese

½ cup grass-fed heavy cream or half and half

¼ to ⅓ cup chopped fresh herbs (optional)

2 teaspoons grated lemon zest

¾ teaspoon fine sea salt

Freshly ground black pepper or dried chile flakes

In a medium bowl, whisk together the ricotta, cream, herbs (if using), lemon zest, salt, and a grind or pinch of pepper. Taste and adjust the seasonings as desired. Spread it on stretched- or rolled-out pizza dough, add toppings, and bake. Refrigerate extra sauce in an airtight container for up to 4 days.

VARIATION TIP: To make Garlicky Ricotta Cream Sauce, heat the heavy cream in a small saucepan over low heat and add 3 to 5 minced garlic cloves. Let the cream heat up just until it begins to steam and you can smell the garlic. Remove the pan from the heat and let cool to room temperature, then whisk in the other ingredients.

PIZZA PAIRINGS: The mild, slightly lemony flavor of this sauce is easily overpowered. Choose tender vegetables like peas, sauteed mushrooms, chives, spinach, and scallions to accentuate the springy vibes, and add cured meat (like bacon) and/or a sprinkle of parmesan or pecorino for a welcome hit of saltiness/umami.

DECONSTRUCTED CREAM "SAUCE" METHOD

This is more of a magic trick than a recipe. Here, instead of mixing together the components of a white sauce, you layer them separately on the pizza. Everything melts into each other in the oven, and another drizzle of cream right after baking amps up the milky flavors, delivering a white sauce that's light, flavorful, and unlike any other.

MAKES 1
(12- TO 14-INCH)
PIZZA

PREP TIME:
5 MINUTES

¼ cup heavy cream

Extra-virgin olive oil

Kosher salt and freshly ground black pepper (or other seasonings)

**SCAN FOR
VIDEO DEMO**

Measure the heavy cream into a small measuring cup or other container with a spout for easy pouring. Stretch or roll out a ball of pizza dough to a 12- to 14-inch round (or whatever shape you like). Brush the dough with a thin layer of olive oil, making sure to get all the way to the edges, sprinkle with salt and pepper, and add your toppings and cheese. Carefully drizzle half of the cream over the toppings, leaving a ½-inch border all around so none of the cream drips over the dough edges. I usually drizzle in a spiral pattern, but zigzags work, too.

Transfer the pizza to the oven and bake until the crust is golden and the bottom is evenly browned. Remove from the oven, transfer to a cutting board, and immediately drizzle with the remaining cream. Let the pizza cool for about 5 minutes, until the cream has congealed into a sauce. Slice and serve.

PIZZA PAIRINGS: This method is best with some sort of allium (scallions, leek, chives, green onions, garlic scapes), salty aged cheese (parmesan, aged cheddar, aged gouda), and cooked chopped bacon (if you want to add meat). Make it that way first (page 170), then experiment with other tender vegetables, cheeses, and cured meats.

TOPPINGS (TO MIX AND MATCH)

The purpose of this book is not to teach you how to make the pizzas *I* like—it's to give you all the info you need to create pizza recipes of your own. In the charts that follow, you'll find a wide variety of pizza-friendly cheeses, fruits, vegetables, and proteins; suggestions on how to prep them as toppings; and lists of other flavors and foods to pair them with. Browse the sections for inspiration or start with one ingredient (a specific cheese, seasonal veggie, or favorite cured meat) and build from there. The pizzabilities are endless!

CHEESES

Yes, mozzarella wins the popularity contest for its unique meltability and mild, milky flavor. However, you're missing out if you don't give other cheeses a chance. Here, I've divided 19 types into three categories based on texture: Softies (chèvre, fresh mozzarella), Semi-Firm Melters (cheddar, jack, low-moisture mozzarella), and Hard/Aged (parmesan, pecorino).

As a general rule, you'll need 4 to 6 ounces of cheese for a "regular" 12- to 14-inch pizza—and double that amount for a sheet pan pizza.

SOFTIES

This category is a mixed bag, including mild, buttery mounds, tangy blocks and logs that crumble to varying degrees, soft spreads, and some real stinkers. What sticks them all together are their soft, sometimes gooey textures. Use them on their own with other toppings, or pair them with hard (aged) cheeses for some extra depth.

TYPE/VARIETY	COMPLEMENTARY TOPPINGS
BRIE Cut into thin slices or squares	Sauces/seasonings: Bacon jam, fig spread, French flavors, fruit preserves, hot honey Other cheeses: Cheddar, mozzarella Veggies/fruits: Apples, arugula and other bitter greens, berries, caramelized onions, cherries, cranberries, dates, fennel, figs, grapes, mushrooms, onions, pears, shallot, tomatoes Meats/proteins: Bacon, cured meats (charcuterie, especially prosciutto), ham, poultry, nuts
BURRATA Tear or cut into bite-size pieces; add after baking	Sauces/seasonings: Balsamic vinegar/glaze (page 114), bruschetta, pesto, tomato sauce Other cheeses: Mozzarella, parmesan, pecorino Veggies/fruits: Arugula, basil, bell peppers, cherries, figs, garlic, olives, peaches/nectarines, strawberries, tender herbs, tomatoes Meats/proteins: Bacon/pancetta, nuts, prosciutto and other cured meats (charcuterie)

FETA Crumble	**Sauces/seasonings:** Cooked tomato sauce, Greek and Mediterranean flavors, honey, lemon, pesto **Other cheeses:** Cheddar, goat, jack, mozzarella **Veggies/fruits:** Basil, bell peppers, dill, eggplant, figs, garlic, melons, mint, olives (especially kalamata), onion, spinach, tender herbs, tomatoes, zucchini/summer squash **Meats/proteins:** Chickpeas, grilled meats, seafood
FRESH GOAT CHEESE (CHÈVRE) Crumble	**Sauces/seasonings:** Balsamic vinegar/glaze (page 114), cream, fruit preserves/spreads, honey, pesto **Other cheeses:** Asiago (aged), feta, Havarti, mozzarella, muenster **Veggies/fruits:** Arugula, apricots, asparagus, basil, beets, bell peppers, blackberries, broccoli, butternut squash/winter squash, caramelized onions, cherries, chives, fennel, figs, garlic, green beans, mushrooms, peas, raspberries, scallions, zucchini/summer squash **Meats/proteins:** Eggs, pecans, prosciutto and other cured meats (charcuterie), grilled steak, walnuts
FRESH MOZZARELLA Cut into ½-inch dice	**Sauces/seasonings:** Balsamic vinegar/glaze (page 114), Italian flavors, olive oil, pesto, tapenade, tomato sauce **Other cheeses:** Aged gouda, cheddar, parmesan, pecorino, provolone, ricotta **Veggies/fruits:** Basil and other tender herbs, bell peppers, eggplant, garlic, olives, tomatoes, vegetables with lower moisture content **Meats/proteins:** Anchovies, pepperoni/salami, other cured meats (charcuterie), sausage
GORGONZOLA/ CREAMY BLUE CHEESES Crumble	**Sauces/seasonings:** Balsamic vinegar/glaze (page 114), cream, fig paste, honey, Italian flavors **Other cheeses:** Jack, mozzarella, mild cheddar, parmesan **Veggies/fruits:** Apples, arugula, cherries, corn, dark leafy greens, dried fruit, figs, olives, pears, pomegranate, potatoes, pumpkin/winter squash, radicchio, spinach **Meats/proteins:** Bacon, nuts, pancetta, prosciutto, steak, walnuts
RACLETTE AND CAMEMBERT Slice	**Sauces/seasonings:** Cream, French flavors **Other cheeses:** Aged gouda, cheddar, fontina, Gruyère, mozzarella **Veggies/fruits:** Asparagus, brussels sprouts, cauliflower, garlic, grapes, green beans, pickles, potatoes, red onion, roasted vegetables, shallot **Meats/proteins:** Bacon, grilled or roasted beef, ham, kielbasa or bratwurst
RICOTTA Dollop	**Sauces/seasonings:** Balsamic vinegar/glaze (page 114), cream, honey, Italian flavors, lemon, pesto, tapenade, tomato sauce **Other cheeses:** Mozzarella, parmesan, pecorino **Veggies/fruits:** Bell peppers, berries, corn, eggplant, figs, herbs (any), peaches/nectarines, scallions, spinach and other tender greens, roasted vegetables, tomatoes, zucchini/summer squash **Meats/proteins:** Bacon, cured meats (charcuterie), eggs, nuts, sausage

SEMI-FIRM MELTERS

These are the reliable, mild-yet-nuanced melters you need for bridging different flavors and textures and securing toppings to slices. Use one as your primary pizza cheese, or create a unique mix using two or three different options. (Write down your favorite cheese combos on page 118 for future reference.)

TYPE/VARIETY	COMPLEMENTARY TOPPINGS
CHEDDAR (MILD) AND YOUNG ASIAGO Shred	Sauces/seasonings: Barbecue sauce, chutney, cream, kimchi, Mexican flavors, quince paste, pepper jelly Other cheeses: Gruyère, mozzarella, parmesan Veggies/fruits: Apples, basil, beets, bell peppers, dark leafy greens, dates, fennel, garlic, grapes, hot (chile) peppers, oregano, pears, pickled vegetables, potatoes, pumpkin/winter squash, tender greens, thyme, zucchini/summer squash Meats/proteins: Bacon, beans, beef, eggs, nuts, prosciutto and other cured meats
FONTINA Shred	Sauces/seasonings: Balsamic vinegar/glaze (page 114), chutney, cream, tomato sauce Other cheeses: Blue (gorgonzola), mozzarella, parmesan Veggies/fruits: Arugula, caramelized onions, garlic, grapes, hot (chile) peppers, mushrooms, olives, pears, tender greens Meats/proteins: Chicken, prosciutto and other cured meats (charcuterie), walnuts
GRUYÈRE Shred	Sauces/seasonings: Balsamic vinegar/glaze (page 114), cream, cooked tomato sauce Other cheeses: Cheddar, Emmentaler, jack, smoked gouda Veggies/fruits: Apples, arugula, asparagus, cherries, chives, dark leafy greens, garlic, grapes, mushrooms, onion (especially caramelized), pears, potatoes, pumpkin/winter squash, root vegetables, spinach Meats/proteins: Bacon, chicken, cured meats (charcuterie), eggs, ham, nuts, sausage
LOW-MOISTURE MOZZARELLA Shred	Sauces/seasonings: Balsamic vinegar/glaze (page 114), Italian flavors, olive oil, pesto, tapenade, tomato sauce Other cheeses: Cheddar, goat, parmesan, pecorino, provolone, ricotta Veggies/fruits: Basil and other tender herbs, bell peppers, eggplant, garlic, hot (chile) peppers, mushrooms, olives, tomatoes, vegetables (almost any) Meats/proteins: Anchovies, cured meats (charcuterie), pepperoni/salami, sausage

MANCHEGO Shred	**Sauces/seasonings:** Chutney, cooked tomato sauce, fig spread, olive oil, quince paste, romesco, Spanish flavors, tomato jam **Other cheeses:** Fresh goat (chèvre) **Veggies/fruits:** Apples, apricots, bell peppers, caramelized onions, dried fruit, figs, grapes (especially red), hot (chile) peppers, olives, parsley, rosemary, sun-dried tomatoes, tender greens, thyme, tomatoes **Meats/proteins:** Anchovies, chorizo, cured meats (charcuterie), ham (especially Serrano), nuts
MONTEREY JACK, COLBY, GOUDA, AND BRICK CHEESE Shred	**Sauces/seasonings:** Barbecue sauce, chili and chili powder, cream, Mexican flavors, ranch dressing, tomato sauce **Other cheeses:** Cheddar, mozzarella **Veggies/fruits:** Basil, bell peppers, broccoli, cauliflower, cilantro, corn, figs, garlic, green beans, hot (chile) peppers, mushrooms, olives, oregano, pickles/preserved veggies, potatoes, spinach, sweet potato, tomatoes, zucchini/summer squash **Meats/proteins:** Bacon, beans, chicken, eggs, meat (any kind, cooked or cured), nuts, sausage
MUENSTER Shred	**Sauces/seasonings:** Caraway, cream, German flavors, mustard **Other cheeses:** Cheddar, goat **Veggies/fruits:** Apples, arugula, caramelized onions, cherries, fennel, grapes, mushrooms, pears, roasted red peppers **Meats/proteins:** Bacon, chicken/turkey, cured meats (charcuterie), ground meat, ham, sausage, steak
PROVOLONE Shred	**Sauces/seasonings:** Bruschetta chili jam, chutney, fig spread, Italian flavors, tomato sauce, pesto **Other cheeses:** Cheddar, mozzarella, Swiss **Veggies/fruits:** Artichokes (canned or jarred), basil and other tender herbs, bell peppers, broccoli rabe, dark leafy greens, dried apricots, eggplant, figs, grapes, hot (chile) peppers, marinated vegetables (such as giardiniera), olives, pears, roasted red peppers, tomatoes, zucchini/summer squash **Meats/proteins:** Cured meats (charcuterie), meatballs, roast beef and pork, sausage

HARD (AGED) CHEESES

Hard, crystalized aged cheeses aren't the best melters, but their concentrated, salty flavors can add depth to pizzas topped with milder cheeses like mozzarella. Try adding ¼ cup finely shredded or grated aged cheese to your next Margherita (page 161) before baking, or experiment with different options from the list below for your own take on Bacon, Leek, and Cream Pizza (page 170).

TYPE/VARIETY	COMPLEMENTARY TOPPINGS
AGED GOUDA AND CHEDDAR Finely shred	**Sauces/seasonings:** Barbecue sauce, cream, fruit spreads (especially apple butter and pepper jelly), onion jam, pesto, tomato sauce **Other cheeses:** Fresh mozzarella, jack and other mild melters, ricotta **Veggies/fruits:** Apples, apricots, bell peppers, broccoli, caramelized onions, cauliflower, cherries, dark leafy greens, hot (chile) peppers, mushrooms, oregano, peaches/nectarines, pears, pumpkin/winter squash, roasted red peppers, rosemary, sage, spinach and other tender greens, thyme **Meats/proteins:** Bacon, beans, cured meats (charcuterie), grilled or roasted meat and poultry, ham
PARMESAN (PARMIGIANO-REGGIANO) Finely shred or grate	**Sauces/seasonings:** Balsamic vinegar/glaze (page 114), cream, honey, Italian flavors, lemon, pesto, tomato sauce **Other cheeses:** Burrata, fresh mozzarella, other Italian cheeses, pecorino, ricotta **Veggies/fruits:** Apples, arugula, basil and other tender herbs, bell peppers, caramelized onions, dark leafy greens, dates, eggplant, fennel, figs, garlic, grapes, green beans, leeks, mushrooms, olives, onion, peas, pears, roasted vegetables, scallions, spinach, tomatoes, zucchini/summer squash **Meats/proteins:** Beans, chicken, nuts, prosciutto and other cured meats (charcuterie), sausage, seafood (especially shrimp and shellfish)
PECORINO AND AGED ASIAGO Finely shred or grate	**Sauces/seasonings:** Balsamic vinegar/glaze (page 114), black pepper, fruit preserves/spreads, honey, Italian flavors, lemon, pesto, tomato sauce **Other cheeses:** Burrata, fresh mozzarella, other Italian cheeses, parmesan, ricotta **Veggies/fruits:** Arugula, asparagus, basil and other tender herbs, bell peppers, broccoli, broccoli rabe, Brussels sprouts, dark leafy greens, eggplant, fennel, grapes, leeks, mushrooms, pears, pumpkin/winter squash, root vegetables, spinach, tomatoes, zucchini/summer squash **Meats/proteins:** Bacon, grilled meat or poultry, ham, cured meats (charcuterie), shrimp, walnuts

FRUITS AND VEGETABLES

Stick to tradition with peppers, onion, mushrooms, olives, etc., or think outside the pizzeria box with fresh corn kernels, asparagus, pumpkin, mango, berries, or apples. Here, you'll find 38 pizza-friendly fruits and vegetables, complete with quantities, prepping instructions, and lists of complementary sauces, proteins, cheeses, and toppings.

As a rule, plan for 1 to 2 cups of prepped fruit/veggie toppings per 12- to 14-inch pizza (2 to 3 cups for a sheet pan pizza).

FRUITS

TYPE	AMOUNT	COMPLEMENTARY TOPPINGS
APPLES Core and thinly slice; add before baking	1 medium	Sauces/seasonings: Barbecue sauce, cinnamon, cream, curry, honey, lemon, maple syrup Meats/proteins: Bacon, cured meats (charcuterie), pork, sausage Other fruits/veggies: Apricots, celeriac, cherries, chives, cranberries, fennel, onion, parsley, pears, pomegranate, pumpkin/winter squash, rosemary, thyme, sauerkraut, sweet potatoes Cheeses: Camembert, cheddar, goat, Gruyère, Swiss/Alpine
APRICOTS Peel, pit, and thinly slice or chop; add before or after baking	2	Sauces/seasonings: Cardamom, cinnamon, cream, honey, lemon, maple syrup Meats/proteins: Almonds, pistachios, pork, poultry, walnuts Other fruits/veggies: Apples, berries, cherries, cranberries, garlic, lemon verbena, mint, onion, rosemary, tender greens Cheeses: Brie, mozzarella, ricotta
FIGS Slice or quarter; add before baking	6 to 8	Sauces/seasonings: Balsamic vinegar/glaze (page 114), cream, honey, lemon, lime Meats/proteins: Almond, anchovies, bacon, ham, pancetta, prosciutto, walnuts Other fruits/veggies: Apples, arugula, garlic, onion, raspberries, rosemary Cheeses: Blue, goat, jack, Manchego, mascarpone, mozzarella, provolone, ricotta

GRAPES, RED SEEDLESS	1 heaping cup	**Sauces/seasonings:** Cream, curry, lemon, paprika **Meats/proteins:** Almonds, pecans, pistachios, prosciutto, roasted pork or poultry, walnuts **Other fruits/veggies:** Endive, garlic, mint, rosemary, tender greens **Cheeses:** Blue, brie, cow's milk, goat's milk
Halve and add before baking		
MANGO Peel and cut flesh into ½-inch dice or thin slices; add before or after baking	1	**Sauces/seasonings:** Balsamic vinegar/glaze (page 114), chili powder, cream, curry, lemon, lime **Meats/proteins:** Bacon, pork, poultry, prosciutto, shrimp, salmon, tuna **Other fruits/veggies:** Avocado, basil, bell peppers, berries, cilantro, hot (chile) peppers, mint, onion, scallions **Cheeses:** Blue, cheddar, goat, Monterey Jack, pepper jack
PEACHES AND NECTARINES Peel, pit, and thinly slice or chop; add before or after baking	1 medium	**Sauces/seasonings:** Balsamic vinegar/glaze (page 114), cinnamon, cream, honey, lemon **Meats/proteins:** Almonds, cured meats (charcuterie), pecans, pistachios, walnuts **Other fruits/veggies:** Apricots, berries, arugula, basil, cherries, hot (chile) peppers, lemon thyme, lemon verbena, mint, onion, tarragon, tender greens **Cheeses:** Goat, mozzarella, ricotta
PEARS Core and thinly slice or chop; add before baking	1 medium or 2 small	**Sauces/seasonings:** Anise, cream, honey, lemon **Meats/proteins:** Almonds, bacon, chestnuts, cured meats (charcuterie), grilled/roasted meats, pistachios, pork **Other fruits/veggies:** Apples, arugula, basil, berries, cherries, cranberries, endive, fennel, figs, mint, pumpkin/winter squash, radicchio, rosemary, scallions, tender greens, watercress **Cheeses:** Blue, brie, camembert, cheddar, feta, goat, jack, mascarpone, parmesan, pecorino, ricotta
PINEAPPLE Discard rind, quarter and core, then chop or cut into ½-inch dice; add before or after baking	½ to 1 cup diced (from ¼ medium fruit)	**Sauces/seasonings:** Chili powder, cream, curry, cooked tomato sauce **Meats/proteins:** Bacon, ham, roasted/grilled meats and poultry, prosciutto and other mild cured meats (charcuterie), shrimp **Other fruits/veggies:** Avocado, basil, bell peppers, cilantro, dried chile flakes, hot

PINEAPPLE Continued		(chile) peppers, mint, onion, rosemary, shallots, spinach and other tender greens, watercress Cheeses: Asiago, blue, Comté, fontina, gouda, mozzarella, parmesan
POMEGRANATE Halve or quarter, then separate the seeds (arils) from the membrane; add after baking	⅓ to ½ cup arils (from 1 whole fruit)	Sauces/seasonings: Balsamic vinegar/glaze (page 114), cream, cumin, lemon Meats/proteins: Roasted/grilled meats, walnuts Other fruits/veggies: Arugula, avocado, beets, hot (chile) peppers, mint, parsley, tender greens Cheeses: Brie, goat, ricotta, smoked or sharp cheddar
SWEET CHERRIES Pit and halve or chop; add before or after baking	1 cup	Sauces/seasonings: Balsamic vinegar/glaze (page 114), cream, lemon Meats/proteins: Almonds, pâté, pork, roasted/grilled meats and poultry, walnuts Other fruits/veggies: Apricots, tender greens Cheeses: Brie, goat, ricotta

VEGETABLES

TYPE	AMOUNT	COMPLEMENTARY TOPPINGS
ASPARAGUS Snap off the tough ends and cut the raw stalks on the diagonal into ¼- to ½-inch-thick pieces, then add with other toppings before baking	½ pound	Sauces/seasonings: Cream, French flavors, pesto, tomato sauce Meats/proteins: Bacon, cold-smoked salmon, eggs, ham, pancetta, pistachios, prosciutto Other veggies/fruits: Basil, dill, garlic, garlic scapes, leeks, mint, mushrooms, parsley, ramps, shallots, tomatoes Cheeses: Burrata, chèvre, fontina, aged goat, mozzarella, muenster, parmesan, pecorino, ricotta
AVOCADO Peel, pit, and cut into ½-inch dice (or mash it with lime or lemon juice, salt, and pepper if you want a guacamole feel); slice the pizza, then scatter or dollop with the avocado just before serving	1	Sauces/seasonings: Balsamic vinegar/glaze (page 114), cream, salsa, tomato sauce Meats/proteins: Bacon, black beans, crab, lobster, shrimp Other veggies/fruits: Arugula, basil, cilantro, corn, garlic, hot (chile) peppers, mango, onion, scallions, tomatoes Cheeses: Blue, feta, goat, jack, mozzarella, sharp cheddar

BEETS Dice and roast (page 103) or boil; add before baking	1 to 2 medium to large	**Sauces/seasonings:** Balsamic vinegar/glaze (page 114), cream, honey, horseradish, lemon, orange **Meats/proteins:** Grilled or roasted meat and poultry, pistachios, walnuts **Other veggies/fruits:** Apples, basil, chives, dill, garlic, mint, onion, parsley, pears, shallots, tarragon **Cheeses:** Blue, cheddar, goat, parmesan
BELL PEPPERS Slice or chop; add before baking	1 small to medium (or ½ large)	**Sauces/seasonings:** Italian flavors, lemon, pesto, salsa, tapenade, tomato sauce **Meats/proteins:** Anchovies, bacon, beef, sausage **Other veggies/fruits:** Basil, eggplant, garlic, hot (chile) peppers, olives, onion, oregano, parsley, thyme, tomatoes, zucchini/summer squash **Cheeses:** Cheddar, feta, fontina, goat, jack, mozzarella, parmesan
BROCCOLI RABE Chop and blanch (page 103); add before baking	½ bunch (about 1 pound)	**Sauces/seasonings:** Balsamic vinegar/glaze (page 114), chimichurri, cream, Italian flavors, pesto, tomato sauce **Meats/proteins:** Almonds, anchovies, chicken, chickpeas, pepperoni/salami, prosciutto, sausage, white beans **Other veggies/fruits:** Basil, chives, dried chile flakes, garlic, hot (chile) peppers, oregano, parsley, piquillo peppers, tomatoes **Cheeses:** Mozzarella, parmesan, pecorino, provolone
BROCCOLI/BROCCOLINI Cut into bite-size florets and blanch (page 103); add before baking	1 pound (1 medium or 2 small heads)	**Sauces/seasonings:** Balsamic vinegar/glaze (page 114), cream, lemon, mustard, pesto, tapenade, tomato sauce **Meats/proteins:** Almonds, anchovies, cured meats (charcuterie), eggs, sausage **Other veggies/fruits:** Basil, capers, dried chile flakes, garlic, hot (chile) peppers, olives, oregano, parsley, scallions, shallots, tarragon, tomatoes **Cheeses:** Cheddar, feta, goat, jack, mozzarella, parmesan, provolone, Swiss/Alpine

BRUSSELS SPROUTS Shred to add raw or halve/quarter and roast (page 103); add before baking	1 pound	**Sauces/seasonings:** Cream, lemon, mustard, Old Bay seasoning, paprika **Meats/proteins:** Bacon, ham, nuts, pancetta, poultry, white beans **Other veggies/fruits:** Apples, celeriac, garlic, onion, parsley, rosemary, thyme **Cheeses:** Blue, cheddar, goat, Gruyère, parmesan, provolone, ricotta, Swiss/Alpine
CARROTS Shred to add raw or dice/slice and roast (page 103) or boil; add before baking	1 to 1½ pounds	**Sauces/seasonings:** Cinnamon, cream, cumin, honey, lemon, lime, maple syrup **Meats/proteins:** Bacon, beef, pistachios, scallops, walnuts **Other veggies/fruits:** Basil, chervil, dill, garlic, hot (chile) peppers, mint, parsley, shallots, spinach and other tender greens, tarragon, thyme **Cheeses:** Cheddar, goat, gouda, parmesan
CAULIFLOWER Cut into bite-size florets and blanch (page 103); add before baking	1 small or ½ medium to large head	**Sauces/seasonings:** Indian, Italian, and Mediterranean flavors; chimichurri, cream, curry powder, lemon, mustard, paprika, pesto, romesco, tomato sauce **Meats/proteins:** Anchovies, cured meats (charcuterie), mussels, walnuts **Other veggies/fruits:** Bell peppers, capers, chives, dill, garlic, greens, hot (chile) peppers, leeks, mint, olives, onion, parsley, rosemary, scallions, shallots, tomatoes, watercress **Cheeses:** Blue, cheddar, goat, Gruyère, parmesan, pecorino
CORN Shuck whole ear and slice raw kernels off cob; add raw before baking	1 ear	**Sauces/seasonings:** Barbecue sauce, chili powder, cream, curry powder, lemon, lime, Mexican flavors, paprika, pesto, tomato sauce **Meats/proteins:** Bacon, beef, clams, crabmeat, eggs, salmon, ham, lobster, pancetta, scallops **Other veggies/fruits:** Basil, bell peppers, chives, cilantro, dill, fennel, garlic, hot (chile) peppers, leeks, lima and fava beans, mushrooms, onion, oregano, parsley, thyme, tomatoes, zucchini/summer squash **Cheeses:** Cheddar, Colby, cotija, feta, jack, mozzarella

DARK LEAFY GREENS (KALE, COLLARD GREENS, SWISS CHARD, ETC.) Chop and blanch (page 103); add before baking	½ bunch (1 to 2 cups shredded or chopped)	**Sauces/seasonings:** Caraway, chili powder, cream, curry, horseradish, lemon, mustard, paprika, tomato sauce **Meats/proteins:** Bacon, eggs, ham, nuts, oysters, shrimp **Other veggies/fruits:** Basil, dried chile flakes, fennel, garlic, leeks, mushrooms, pears, pomegranate, scallions, tomatoes, winter squash **Cheeses:** Asiago, jack, parmesan
EGGPLANT Slice or chop and roast just until soft (page 103); add before baking	1 small to medium	**Sauces/seasonings:** Chili powder, chimichurri, cinnamon, curry powder, lemon, miso, pesto, romesco, sumac, tomato sauce **Meats/proteins:** Anchovies, chickpeas, Italian sausage, pine nuts, prosciutto **Other veggies/fruits:** Basil, bell peppers, capers, chives, cilantro, dried chile flakes, fennel, garlic, hot (chile) peppers, mint, mushrooms, olives, onion, oregano, parsley, pomegranate, rosemary, scallions, zucchini/summer squash, tomatoes **Cheeses:** Emmental, feta, goat, Gruyère, mozzarella, parmesan, pecorino, ricotta, Swiss/Alpine
FENNEL Slice thinly; add raw before baking	½ to 1 bulb	**Sauces/seasonings:** Cream, lemon, orange, pesto, tomato sauce **Meats/proteins:** Almonds, chicken, crabmeat, cured meats (charcuterie), lobster, salmon, shrimp, tuna, walnuts **Other veggies/fruits:** Apples, arugula, asparagus, beets, garlic, herbs, olives, pears, tomatoes, zucchini/summer squash **Cheeses:** Blue, goat, Gruyère, mozzarella, parmesan, pecorino
GARLIC Peel and chop or slice thinly to add raw, or roast whole head (page 103) and squeeze out cloves; add before baking	2 to 3 cloves if adding raw, 1 head if roasting	**Sauces/seasonings:** Balsamic vinegar/glaze (page 114), barbecue, cream, curry, Italian flavors, lemon, pesto, tomato sauce **Meats/proteins:** Anchovies, bacon, beans, beef, cured meats (charcuterie), chicken, eggs, nuts, pork, shrimp **Other veggies/fruits:** Basil, beets, broccoli, broccoli rabe, eggplant, fennel, green beans, greens, hot (chile) peppers, herbs, leeks, mushrooms, onion, spinach, tomatoes, zucchini/summer squash **Cheeses:** Goat, mozzarella, parmesan, pecorino, provolone

GARLIC SCAPES	3 to 5	**Sauces/seasonings:** Balsamic vinegar/glaze (page 114), barbecue, cream, curry, lemon
Trim and blanch (page 103) or sauté just until al dente; add before baking		**Meats/proteins:** Anchovies, bacon, beans, chicken, cured meats (charcuterie), eggs, seafood
		Other veggies/fruits: Basil, beets, broccoli, eggplant, fennel, herbs (especially Italian), hot (chile) peppers, leeks, mushrooms, onion, spinach and other tender greens, tomatoes, zucchini/summer squash
		Cheeses: Goat, mozzarella, parmesan, pecorino, provolone
GREEN BEANS	½ pound	**Sauces/seasonings:** Cream, cumin, lemon, paprika, pesto, tomato sauce
Trim and slice on the diagonal to add raw, blanch (page 103), or sauté in a little olive oil just until bright green; add before baking.		**Meats/proteins:** Almonds, anchovies, bacon, eggs, ham, prosciutto, shrimp, walnuts
		Other veggies/fruits: Apples, basil, bell peppers, capers, chives, dill, garlic, hot (chile) peppers, marjoram, olives, onion, parsley, potatoes, shallots, tarragon, thyme, tomatoes
		Cheeses: Asiago, blue, feta, goat, parmesan
GREEN PEAS (FRESH OR FROZEN)	1 to 1½ cups	**Sauces/seasonings:** Cream, lemon, no-cook tomato sauce, pesto
Blanch (page 103); add before baking		**Meats/proteins:** Bacon, crabmeat, ham, prosciutto
		Other veggies/fruits: Arugula, basil, chervil, chives, dill, garlic, hot (chile) peppers, leeks, mint, mushrooms, onion, parsley, scallions, shallots, spinach and other tender greens, tarragon, thyme, tomatoes
		Cheeses: Cheddar, fontina, goat, mozzarella, parmesan, Swiss/Alpine
HOT (CHILE) PEPPERS	1 to 2, depending on heat level and preference	**Sauces/seasonings:** Cream, cumin, curry powder, lemon, lime, pesto, salsa, tomato sauce
Remove the seeds (or leave some in for extra heat) and chop or slice into thin rings; add raw before or after baking		**Meats/proteins:** Beans, cured meats (charcuterie), poultry, sausage, seafood
		Other veggies/fruits: Avocado, basil, cilantro, corn, eggplant, fennel, garlic, mango, mushrooms, onion, pineapple, tomatoes
		Cheeses: Cheddar, feta, fontina, goat, jack, mozzarella, parmesan

LEEKS Trim off the root and tough, dark-green end; cut in half lengthwise, slice thinly, and wash well in a colander under running water, separating the layers. Add raw before baking.	1 medium to large	**Sauces/seasonings:** Balsamic vinegar/glaze (page 114), cream, mustard, no-cook tomato sauce **Meats/proteins:** Anchovies, bacon, chicken, eggs **Other veggies/fruits:** Chives, garlic, oregano, potatoes, scallions, tarragon, thyme, tomatoes **Cheeses:** Aged gouda, cheddar, goat, Gruyère, parmesan, Swiss/Alpine
MUSHROOMS Stem and thinly slice; sauté just until tender or add raw to pizza before baking.	½ to 1 pound	**Sauces/seasonings:** Balsamic vinegar/glaze (page 114), cream, lemon, pesto, tomato sauce **Meats/proteins:** Bacon, chicken, crabmeat, eggs, ham, prosciutto **Other veggies/fruits:** Asparagus, bell peppers, capers, chives, fennel, garlic, green beans, hot (chile) peppers, herbs, leeks, marjoram, onion, parsley, peas, rosemary, scallions, shallots, spinach and other tender greens, tarragon, thyme, tomatoes **Cheeses:** Asiago, cheddar, Gruyère, mozzarella, parmesan, pecorino, Swiss/Alpine
ONIONS Mince, chop, or thinly slice; sauté, caramelize (page 104), or use raw; add before baking	1 small to medium	**Sauces/seasonings:** Balsamic vinegar/glaze (page 114), cream, pesto, tapenade, tomato sauce **Meats/proteins:** Anchovies, bacon, cured meats (charcuterie), grilled/roasted beef and pork **Other veggies/fruits:** Beets, bell peppers, herbs, garlic, hot (chile) peppers, mushrooms, olives, vegetables (in general) **Cheeses:** Blue, cheddar, goat, Gruyère, parmesan, Swiss/Alpine
PARSNIPS, SWEET POTATOES/YAMS, AND OTHER ROOT VEGETABLES Peel, slice or chop into ½-inch pieces, and roast (page 103); add before baking.	1 to 1½ pounds	**Sauces/seasonings:** Balsamic vinegar/glaze (page 114), cinnamon, cream, curry, maple syrup, pesto, tomato sauce **Meats/proteins:** Bacon, beans, eggs, grilled and roasted meat **Other veggies/fruits:** Apples, chives, fennel, garlic, dark leafy greens, mushrooms, parsley, rosemary, shallots, thyme **Cheeses:** Cheddar, fontina, gouda, Gruyère, jack, Swiss/Alpine

POTATOES	1 to 1½ pounds	**Sauces/seasonings:** Cream, mustard, paprika, pesto
Peel and cut into paper-thin slices, soak in salt water for 1 hour, then drain, pat dry, toss with olive oil, and add before baking; alternatively, boil the sliced potatoes for 2 minutes (until just al dente), then drain well, pat dry, and add before baking. (See Potato Pizza recipe, page 172)		**Meats/proteins:** Bacon, corned beef, cured meats (charcuterie), roasted or grilled beef **Other veggies/fruits:** Arugula, celeriac, chives, garlic, dark leafy greens, hot (chile) peppers, leeks, mushrooms, onion, parsley, rosemary, shallots, sorrel, thyme, tomatoes, truffle **Cheeses:** Blue, cheddar, fontina, goat, gouda, Gruyère, jack, Manchego, mozzarella, parmesan, pecorino, raclette
PUMPKIN AND WINTER SQUASH	1 to 1½ pounds	**Sauces/seasonings:** Cinnamon, cream, lemon, tomato sauce
Remove hard skin, scoop out seeds, and cut into ¼- to ½-inch-thick slices; roast just until tender (page 103), then add before baking		**Meats/proteins:** Bacon, cured meats (charcuterie), lobster, nuts, oysters, sausage **Other veggies/fruits:** Apples, cranberries, garlic, hot (chile) peppers, mushrooms, onion, radicchio, rosemary, thyme **Cheeses:** Cheddar, feta, gouda, Gruyère, parmesan, pecorino, Swiss/Alpine
SCALLIONS/SPRING ONIONS AND SPRING GARLIC	½ to 1 bunch	**Sauces/seasonings:** Anise, chili, cream, paprika, pesto, tomato sauce
Remove roots and dark green ends. Slice crosswise or lengthwise into ribbons and add to pizza before baking; finely slice or chop to add as garnish after baking.		**Meats/proteins:** Bacon, beans, cured meats (charcuterie), eggs, ham **Other veggies/fruits:** Basil, bell peppers, garlic, hot (chile) peppers, mushrooms, parsley, tomatoes **Cheeses:** Cheddar, goat, gouda, Gruyère, mozzarella, parmesan
TENDER GREENS (SPINACH, ARUGULA, WATERCRESS, ETC.)	3 cups if sautéing, 2 cups if adding raw before baking, 1 cup if adding raw after baking	**Sauces/seasonings:** Balsamic vinegar/glaze (page 114), cream, lemon, pesto, tomato sauce
Sauté in a little olive oil just until wilted and add before baking, add raw under other toppings before baking, or chop and add as garnish after baking		**Meats/proteins:** Bacon, cured meats (charcuterie), eggs, nuts **Other veggies/fruits:** Apples, capers, fennel, garlic, mushrooms, olives, onions, peaches/nectarines, pears, scallions, shallots **Cheeses:** Asiago, feta, goat, gouda, Gruyère, mozzarella, parmesan, ricotta

TOMATOES Slice or chop (use sparingly and scoop out seeds first if combining with other wet toppings); add before or after baking	2 small, 1 medium to large, or 1 cup cherry tomatoes	**Sauces/seasonings:** Balsamic vinegar/glaze (page 114), cream, Italian seasonings, pesto, tomato sauce **Meats/proteins:** Anchovies, beans, cured meats (charcuterie), grilled and roasted meat and poultry, seafood, tofu **Other veggies/fruits:** Arugula, avocado, basil, bell peppers, chives, cilantro, dark leafy greens, dried chile flakes, fennel, garlic, green beans, hot (chile) peppers, leeks, mango, melons, mint, mushrooms, olives, onion, parsley, peas, pineapple, shallots, squash, tender greens, thyme, zucchini/summer squash **Cheeses:** Blue, cheddar, feta, goat, gouda, mozzarella, parmesan, pecorino, ricotta, sheep's milk
ZUCCHINI AND SUMMER SQUASH Slice or chop and keep raw, roast (page 103), or sauté just until soft; add before baking.	1 small	**Sauces/seasonings:** Balsamic vinegar/glaze (page 114), cream, lemon, pesto, tomato sauce **Meats/proteins:** Chorizo, cured meats (charcuterie), Italian sausage, seafood, meats, nuts **Other veggies/fruits:** Basil, bell pepper, chives, cilantro, corn, dried chile flakes, eggplant, garlic, hot (chile) peppers, marjoram, olives, onion, oregano, parsley, scallions, shallots, thyme, tomatoes **Cheeses:** Cheddar, feta, goat, Gruyère, mozzarella, parmesan, pecorino, queso fresco, ricotta

BASIC COOKING TECHNIQUES FOR VEGGIE TOPPINGS

To blanch vegetables:

Slice or chop the vegetables into bite-size pieces. Bring a large pot of water to a boil, carefully add the vegetables, and cook for 30 seconds to 2 minutes, just until they brighten in color and begin to soften. Immediately drain the vegetables in a colander, then dump them into a bowl of ice water to lock in the vibrant color and stop the cooking. Drain and pat dry before using as a pizza topping.

To roast vegetables:

Preheat the oven to 400°F and line a large rimmed baking sheet with parchment paper or aluminum foil. Cut the vegetable(s) into small (roughly ½-inch) pieces, put them in a bowl, and toss them with a drizzle of **extra-virgin olive oil**, a **big pinch or two of kosher salt**, and a **few grinds of black pepper**. Spread the seasoned vegetables in a single layer on the baking sheet. Roast for 15 to 30 minutes, stirring occasionally, until they are tender all the way through and just beginning to brown around the edges. Remove from the oven and let cool before using as a pizza topping.

To roast garlic:

Preheat the oven to 400°F. Remove any excess papery skin from **1 head of garlic**, then slice about ½ inch off the top of the head, exposing the cloves. Place the garlic head cut-side up on a large square of aluminum foil, season with a **pinch of salt** and a **grind or two of black pepper**, and drizzle the exposed cloves with **extra-virgin olive oil**. Fold up the edges of the foil to make a pouch, then place it on a baking sheet. Roast for 40 minutes to 1 hour, until the garlic cloves are very soft. Remove from the oven and set aside to cool, then carefully open the foil pouch and squeeze the soft garlic cloves into a bowl (or remove them with a tip of a small knife if you want the cloves intact).

To caramelize onions:

Slice **2 medium yellow onions**. Melt **3 tablespoons unsalted butter** in a large Dutch oven or wide, heavy skillet over medium heat. Add the onion slices and **2 big pinches of kosher salt**, stir until all the onion slices are coated in butter, and cook for 10 minutes, stirring occasionally. Reduce the heat to medium-low and cook for 30 to 45 minutes, stirring every 5 minutes or so and reducing the heat as needed, until the onions have softened and turned a deep amber color. Remove from the heat and let cool before using as a pizza topping. (Makes about 1 cup.)

PROTEINS

Whether or not meat's your thing, I've got you covered. Add a little extra oomph to your pizzas with plant-based proteins, seafood, poultry, beef, and pork. As with the other topping categories, I've included the amounts you need for a 12- to 14-inch pizza, how to prep each type of protein, and what it can be paired with. Remember: For a "regular" size pizza, all you need is a ½ cup of sauce, 4 to 6 ounces of cheese, and 1 to 2 cups total of other toppings (produce and/or protein).

VEGAN AND VEGETARIAN PROTEINS

TYPE	AMOUNT	COMPLEMENTARY TOPPINGS
BLACK BEANS, CANNED OR COOKED Drain, rinse, and pat dry	1 (15-ounce) can or 1 to 1½ cups	Sauces/seasonings: Lemon, lime, Mexican/Spanish flavors, salsa, tomato sauce Veggies/fruits: Avocado, bell peppers, cilantro, garlic, hot (chile) peppers, onions, parsley, scallions, spinach, sweet potato, tomatoes, winter squash Cheeses: Cheddar, feta, parmesan, smoked gouda or cheddar Other proteins: Bacon, chicken/poultry, chorizo, cured meats (charcuterie)
CHICKPEAS, CANNED OR COOKED Drain, rinse, and pat dry	1 (15-ounce) can or 1 to 1½ cups	Sauces/seasonings: Chimichurri, cumin, lemon, paprika, pesto, romesco, tomato sauce Veggies/fruits: Carrots, cilantro, garlic, hot (chile) peppers, leeks, mint, olives, onion, parsley, spinach, tomatoes Cheeses: Cheddar, feta, fresh goat (chèvre), jack, mozzarella Other proteins: Chicken, shrimp
EGGS Crack into ramekins, then carefully slide onto topped dough before baking	4 to 5	Sauces/seasonings: Cream, paprika, pesto, tomato sauce Veggies/fruits: Asparagus, chives, dill, garlic, leeks, mushrooms, scallions, spinach, tomatoes Cheeses: Cheddar, feta, Gruyère, Havarti, mozzarella, parmesan Other proteins: Bacon, chorizo, ham, smoked salmon, sausage

LIMA AND FAVA BEANS, CANNED OR FRESH Drain, rinse, and pat dry if canned; blanch, shock in an ice bath, and pat dry if fresh	1 cup	Sauces/seasonings: Lemon, Mediterranean flavors, no-cook tomato sauce, olive oil Veggies/fruits: Basil, garlic, mint, scallions Cheeses: Feta, Manchego, parmesan, pecorino, ricotta, sheep's milk Other proteins: Cured meats (charcuterie), ham, seafood
TOFU, FIRM OR EXTRA-FIRM Cut into ½-inch dice	1 (14-ounce) block	Sauces/seasonings: Barbecue sauce, miso, teriyaki sauce, tikka masala sauce, pesto, romesco, tomato sauce Veggies/fruits: Asparagus, bell peppers, eggplant, garlic, hot (chile) peppers, mushrooms, scallions Other proteins: Beans, nuts
WHITE BEANS, CANNED OR COOKED Drain, rinse, and pat dry	1 (15-ounce) can or 1 to 1½ cups	Sauces/seasonings: Balsamic vinegar/glaze (page 114), cream, Italian flavors, lemon, pesto, tomato sauce Veggies/fruits: Arugula, basil, broccoli rabe, chives, fennel, garlic, hot (chile) peppers, mushrooms, onion, parsley Cheeses: Manchego, parmesan, pecorino, Swiss/Alpine Other proteins: Bacon, ham, prosciutto, sausage

SEAFOOD

TYPE	AMOUNT	COMPLEMENTARY TOPPINGS
ANCHOVIES, TINNED, PACKED IN OIL Wipe off excess oil; slice or keep whole, depending on size, and add before baking	4 to 8 fillets	Sauces/seasonings: Lemon, olive oil, pesto, tomato sauce Veggies/fruits: Basil, broccoli, Brussels sprouts, capers, cauliflower, cilantro, fennel, garlic, mint, olives, onion, parsley, tender greens, tomatoes Cheeses: Manchego, mozzarella, parmesan, pecorino Other proteins: Bacon, beans, cured meats (charcuterie), nuts
CLAMS, OYSTERS, AND MUSSELS, CANNED/TINNED Drain and add before baking	1 (6.5-ounce) can or 1 to 2 (3-ounce) tins	Sauces/seasonings: Cream, lemon, olive oil, tomato sauce Veggies/fruits: Basil, chives, fennel, garlic, hot (chile) peppers, leeks, onion, parsley, shallots, spinach, tomatoes

CLAMS, OYSTERS, AND MUSSELS, CANNED/TINNED Continued		Cheeses: Blue, mozzarella, parmesan Other proteins: Bacon, cured meats (charcuterie)
LUMP CRABMEAT AND LOBSTER, CANNED OR REFRIGERATED/FROZEN AND THAWED Drain and add before baking	6 to 8 ounces	Sauces/seasonings: Citrus, cream, Old Bay seasoning, tomato sauce Veggies/fruits: Avocado, basil, bell pepper, chives, cilantro, corn, fennel, garlic, hot (chile) peppers, leeks, mint, mushrooms, onion, parsley, scallions, shallots, tarragon, tomatoes Cheeses: Cheddar, Gruyère, mozzarella, parmesan Other proteins: Eggs
SALMON, COLD-SMOKED (LOX) Slice thinly; add after baking	4 to 6 ounces	(Same as hot-smoked salmon)
SALMON, HOT-SMOKED, COOKED, OR CANNED Flake and add before baking.	4 to 6 ounces	Sauces/seasonings: Cream, lemon, horseradish, pesto Veggies/fruits: Artichokes, avocado, bell peppers, capers, celeriac, chives, dill, garlic, leeks, onion, parsley, shallots, tomatoes Cheeses: Feta, goat's milk, mascarpone Other proteins: Eggs
SCALLOPS Halve or slice, depending on size; add during the last 3-ish minutes of baking (let them cook until just opaque)	½ to 1 pound	Sauces/seasonings: Citrus, cream, French flavors, pesto, tomato sauce Veggies/fruits: Arugula, avocado, bell peppers, chives, cilantro, corn, fennel, garlic, hot (chile) peppers, leeks, mushrooms, parsley, pineapple, pomegranate, scallions, shallots, spinach and other tender greens Cheeses: Gruyère, Comté, mozzarella, parmesan Other proteins: Bacon, beans, cured meats (charcuterie)
SHRIMP AND PRAWNS Peel and cook just until opaque; add whole or chopped before baking	½ to 1 pound	Sauces/seasonings: Balsamic vinegar/glaze (page 114), citrus, cream, curry powder, horseradish, Old Bay seasoning, pesto, tomato sauce Veggies/fruits: Arugula, avocado, basil, bell peppers, celeriac, chives, cilantro, fennel, garlic, green beans, hot (chile)

SHRIMP AND PRAWNS Continued		peppers, mango, mint, mushrooms, onions, parsley, pineapple, radishes, scallions, shallots, tomatoes **Cheeses:** Asiago, feta, goat's milk, parmesan, pecorino **Other proteins:** Bacon, beans, cured meats (charcuterie), nuts
TUNA OR SALMON, CANNED Flake and add before baking	1 (5-ounce) can	**Sauces/seasonings:** Citrus, cream, Mediterranean flavors, olive oil, tomato sauce **Veggies/fruits:** Avocado, basil, bell peppers, chives, cilantro, fennel, garlic, hot (chile) peppers, mushrooms, olives, onion, parsley, radishes, scallions, tomatoes **Cheeses:** Cheddar, Gruyère, jack, mozzarella, parmesan, provolone **Other proteins:** Anchovies, beans, eggs

MEAT AND POULTRY

TYPE	AMOUNT	COMPLEMENTARY TOPPINGS
BACON, PANCETTA, AND PORK BELLY Chop and cook until just beginning to crisp around the edges; add before baking	½ pound	**Sauces/seasonings:** Barbecue sauce, cream, maple syrup, tomato sauce **Veggies/fruits:** Apples, arugula, avocado, green beans, mushrooms, onion, pears, peas, pineapple, potato, root vegetables, shallots, spinach and other tender greens, tomatoes, winter squash, zucchini/summer squash **Cheeses:** Aged gouda, blue, cheddar, Gruyère, jack, mozzarella, muenster **Other proteins:** Beans, chicken, cured meats (charcuterie), eggs, sausage
BEEF AND BISON Cook ground meat just until it's no longer pink; if using steak, add very thin slices raw or cook until medium-rare, slice, and add before baking	1 to 2 cups cooked and crumbled, chopped, or shredded (½ pound)	**Sauces/seasonings:** Balsamic vinegar/glaze (page 114), barbecue sauce, cream, horseradish, tomato sauce **Veggies/fruits:** Arugula, basil, bell peppers, capers, caramelized onions, chard, chives, garlic, hot (chile) peppers, mushrooms, onion, roasted vegetables, scallions, shallots **Cheeses:** Blue, cheddar, fontina, parmesan, provolone, smoked gouda **Other proteins:** Beans, chicken, pork

CHICKEN AND TURKEY Cook and shred or cut into small pieces; add before baking	1 to 2 cups cooked and crumbled, chopped, or shredded (½ pound)	Sauces/seasonings: Balsamic vinegar/glaze (page 114), barbecue sauce, chimichurri, citrus, cream, curry powder, garam masala, paprika, pesto, tomato sauce Veggies/fruits: Artichokes, basil, bell peppers, broccoli, chives, cilantro, dill, greens, garlic, hot (chile) peppers, leeks, mushrooms, olives, onion, parsley, root vegetables, rosemary, sage, shallots, tarragon, tomatoes Cheeses: Asiago, blue, cheddar, Comté, fontina, Gruyère, parmesan Other proteins: Bacon, beans, cured meats (charcuterie), nuts
CORNED BEEF AND PASTRAMI Dice or slice and cut into small squares; add before baking	3 to 4 ounces	Sauces/seasonings: Horseradish, mustard, Russian or Thousand Island dressing Veggies/fruits: Carrots, fennel, pickles, root vegetables, potatoes, sauerkraut Cheeses: Gruyère, muenster, Swiss/Alpine Other proteins: Chicken, ham, roast beef
FRESH CHORIZO SAUSAGE Peel off casings, pinch into small pieces, and cook until it's no longer pink; add before baking	½ pound (2 links)	Sauces/seasonings: Chimichurri, cream, hot honey, Spanish flavors, tomato sauce Veggies/fruits: Apples, bell pepper, butternut squash (and other winter squashes), dried chile flakes, garlic, herbs, hot (chile) peppers, kale, olives (especially Spanish), onion, potatoes, scallions, tomatoes Cheeses: Cheddar, jack, Manchego, sheep's milk Other proteins: Beans, chicken, clams, eggs, shrimp
FRESH ITALIAN SAUSAGE Peel off casings, pinch into small pieces, and cook until it's no longer pink; add before baking	½ pound (2 links)	Sauces/seasonings: Hot honey, Italian flavors, pesto, tomato sauce Veggies/fruits: Apples, arugula, basil, bell peppers, broccoli rabe, dried chile flakes, fennel, garlic, herbs (especially Italian), hot (chile) peppers, mushrooms, oregano, shallots, spinach and other tender greens, tomatoes Cheeses: Mozzarella, parmesan, pecorino, provolone Other proteins: Cured meats (charcuterie), eggs, ham, white beans

HAM AND CANADIAN BACON Cut into ½-inch dice or slice; add before baking	4 to 6 ounces	**Sauces/seasonings:** Barbecue sauce, cream, maple syrup, mustard, tomato sauce **Veggies/fruits:** Apples, arugula, chives, corn, green beans, greens, mushrooms, parsley, peas, pineapple, scallions, spinach and other tender greens, thyme **Cheeses:** Cheddar, Emmental, fontina, Gruyère, jack, Manchego, mozzarella, parmesan, Swiss/Alpine **Other proteins:** Bacon, cured meats (charcuterie), eggs
MEATBALLS Cook and cut in half or quarters, depending on size; add before baking	8 to 10 medium	**Sauces/seasonings:** Italian flavors, pesto, tomato sauce **Veggies/fruits:** Arugula, basil, dried chile flakes, hot (chile) peppers, mint, oregano, spinach, tomatoes **Cheeses:** Cheddar, gouda, mozzarella, parmesan, pecorino **Other proteins:** Cured meats (charcuterie)
'NDUJA (SPREADABLE) SALAMI Dollop on dough before baking	2 ounces (¼ cup)	**Sauces/seasonings:** Tomato sauce **Veggies/fruits:** Basil, broccoli, broccoli rabe, cabbage, fennel, kale, tomatoes **Cheeses:** Blue, goat and sheep's milk, mozzarella, parmesan, pecorino, scamorza **Other proteins:** Beans, chicken, cured meats (charcuterie)
PEPPERONI AND OTHER TYPES OF SALAMI (SOPPRESSATA, GENOA SALAMI, CHORIZO, ETC.) Thinly slice; add before baking (If you want pepperoni to cup up in the oven, start with a pepperoni stick and slice it yourself.)	4 to 5 ounces	**Sauces/seasonings:** Hot honey, Italian flavors, pesto, tomato sauce **Veggies/fruits:** Arugula, basil, bell peppers, broccoli, broccoli rabe, garlic, garlic scapes, hot (chile) peppers, mushrooms, olives, onion, scallions **Cheeses:** Jack, Manchego, mozzarella, parmesan, pecorino, provolone **Other proteins:** Beans, sausage

PROSCIUTTO, MORTADELLA, CAPICOLA, AND OTHER SIMILAR ITALIAN CURED MEATS Thinly slice; tear or chop and arrange under other toppings before baking, or lay on top of the pizza after baking	2 to 4 ounces	**Sauces/seasonings:** Balsamic vinegar/glaze (page 114), Italian and Mediterranean flavors, lemon, olive oil, pesto, tomato sauce **Veggies/fruits:** Arugula, asparagus, basil, fennel, figs, melon, peaches/nectarines, spinach, tomatoes **Cheeses:** Fontina, Gruyère, parmesan, provolone **Other proteins:** Beans, chicken, eggs, nuts, sausage
PULLED PORK Shred or chop; add before baking	1 to 2 cups	**Sauces/seasonings:** Barbecue sauce, chimichurri, cumin, lemon, pesto, tomato sauce **Veggies/fruits:** Bell peppers, garlic, hot (chile) peppers, pineapple, onion, tomatoes **Cheeses:** cheddar, Jack, provolone, Swiss/Alpine **Other proteins:** Bacon, baked beans
SCRAPPLE Slice and cook over medium-high heat; add before baking.	½ pound	**Sauces/seasonings:** Apple butter, cream, ketchup, maple syrup, Old Bay seasoning **Veggies/fruits:** Apples, arugula, chives, parsley, potatoes, scallions **Cheeses:** Cheddar, cooper sharp, gouda, smoked cheddar or gouda **Other proteins:** Bacon, eggs
SPAM Cut into ½-inch dice; add before baking	1 (12-ounce) can	**Sauces/seasonings:** Cream, Hawaiian flavors, Thousand Island dressing **Veggies/fruits:** Chives, hot (chile) peppers, olives, onion, pickles, pineapple, sauerkraut **Cheeses:** American, cheddar, jack, provolone, Swiss/Alpine **Other proteins:** Eggs

NEED MORE TOPPING INSPIRATION?

SEASONINGS, GARNISHES, AND CONDIMENTS

You've stretched or rolled out your dough, added sauce, cheese, and other toppings, and baked the pizza to crispy-on-the-outside, chewy-on-the-inside perfection. Now what? Though of course it's completely fine to slice and serve it unadorned, fresh garnishes, seasonings, and condiments can take homemade pizza from yum to yowza! Sprinkle or drizzle them on pizzas fresh from the oven, or serve them at the table so everyone can personalize their own slices.

SEASONINGS AND GARNISHES

Just like other dishes, homemade pizza benefits from added seasonings and flourishes, both before and after baking. Experiment with the options I've listed here, and explore your spice cabinet for more ideas, noting the best combinations on the notebook pages at the end of this chapter.

BLACK PEPPER, freshly ground, of course, adds depth and zippy spice to sauces, cheeses, vegetables, and meats. Grind some over the pizza before and after baking for multiple levels of flavor.

KOSHER SALT is my preferred choice for seasoning pizza because the larger crystals really hold their own among all the other flavors/toppings. If you have some on hand, **flaked sea salt** also works well.

CAJUN AND MEXICAN SPICE BLENDS (or your favorite dried spice mixes) are easy ways to amp up beans and roasted veggies/meats or personalize simple white- and red-sauce pizzas.

GROUND SUMAC, CHILI POWDER, PAPRIKA, GARLIC POWDER, AND ONION POWDER are all useful for enhancing/accentuating the flavors of pizza toppings before baking.

PIZZA SEASONING is an obvious choice, now available from many different spice companies and usually containing salt, ground black pepper and fennel seeds, dried basil and oregano, powdered garlic and onion, and dried red chile flakes.

DRIED CHILE FLAKES (red pepper flakes, urfa pepper, etc.) add a subtle (or not so subtle) kick to mild, rich, or creamy pizzas.

DRIED HERB BLENDS (like Italian seasoning or herbes de Provence) can be sprinkled into pizza doughs and sauces for some deep, herbaceous flavor, are great seasonings for roasted vegetable and protein toppings, and give finished pizzas a little oomph after baking.

FRESH HERBS, SCALLIONS, AND TENDER GREENS are my favorite garnishes for finished pizzas. Not only do they bring welcome pops of color, but they also add contrasting crunchy/leafy textures and vibrant flavor to each bite.

DIPPERS AND DRIZZLERS

Condiments aren't just for burgers and hot dogs; they can also take fresh-baked pizza to a whole new level. Here are some of the most popular sauces pizza lovers use to liven up slices and crusts.

BALSAMIC GLAZE/REDUCTION is delicious drizzled over fresh-baked white and Margherita pizzas, as well as any pizzas topped with Italian cured meats, spinach/arugula, or roasted/grilled vegetables. See page 114 to learn how to make it yourself.

BARBECUE SAUCE makes a great alternative to "regular" red pizza sauce (especially with corn, green peppers, and bacon or pulled pork toppings), and it's also a great dip for crust.

GARLIC BUTTER is easy to make (see page 114 for directions) and super versatile. Brush it on dough as a sauce, drizzle it over finished pizzas, and serve it at the table for dipping slices and crusts.

HOT SAUCE is best on simple red sauce pizzas like "Plain" Cheese Pizza (page 162) and Margherita (page 161), and on rich pizzas like Meat Lover's (page 166).

HOT HONEY OR GARLIC-INFUSED HONEY adds a welcome sweet-hot note when drizzled over classic plain and pepperoni pizzas hot from the oven.

RANCH DRESSING goes well with just about any red sauce pizza, can be used as a sauce (especially for dill pickle pizza with mozzarella cheese), and is my all-time favorite dip for crust.

FLAVORED/INFUSED OLIVE OILS can elevate just about any pizza. Buy an assortment and experiment with complementary toppings (for example, drizzle lemony olive oil over Pizza Margherita, chile-infused oil over meat pizzas, and herb-infused olive oils over vegetable pizzas).

HERB OIL AND PESTO are classic pizza sauces (see page 82 for recipes), but they're just as good for finishing. Drizzle some over freshly baked pizzas and/or serve it in a small ramekin so guests can use it as a dip.

TO MAKE YOUR OWN GARLIC BUTTER: Grate **4 or 5 medium (or 3 large) garlic cloves** with a zester or the fine holes on your box grater. Melt **1 stick of high-quality unsalted butter** in a small skillet or saucepan over medium heat. Add the grated garlic, reduce the heat to medium-low, and stir for 2 to 3 minutes, then season with a **big pinch of kosher salt**. If you want, squeeze in a little **fresh lemon juice** to taste and add a few grinds of **black pepper**. Pour into a ramekin and serve with homemade pizza for drizzling and dunking.

TO MAKE YOUR OWN BALSAMIC GLAZE: Pour **½ cup of balsamic vinegar** into a small (preferably nonstick or heavy-bottomed) saucepan. Place the pan over medium heat. When it begins to bubble around the edges, reduce the heat to medium-low and let it simmer gently, stirring frequently with a wooden spoon or silicone-coated whisk until the vinegar reduces by about half and has thickened to a syrupy consistency, about 10 minutes. Pour the glaze into a ramekin or other heatproof container and let cool to room temperature. Drizzle over fresh-baked pizza, or place the ramekin on the table with a small spoon and let guests garnish their slices as desired. Store extra glaze in an airtight container in the refrigerator for up to 1 month. (Makes about ¼ cup.)

DESIGN YOUR PERFECT PIZZAS

TOPPINGS THAT WORKED

▶

▶

▶

▶

▶

▶

▶

▶

▶

▶

▶

▶

▶

▶

▶

▶

▶

▶

▶

▶

▶

TOPPING COMBOS TO TRY

▶

▶

▶

▶

▶

▶

▶

▶

▶

▶

▶

▶

▶

▶

▶

▶

▶

▶

▶

▶

▶

▶

FAVORITE PIZZA RECIPES

RECIPE TITLE: _____

MAKES _____ PIZZA(S)

INGREDIENTS

DOUGH: _____   _____

_____   _____

_____   _____

SAUCE: _____   _____

_____   _____

_____   _____

_____   _____

TOPPINGS: _____   _____

_____   _____

_____   _____

DIRECTIONS

_____

_____

_____

_____

_____

_____

_____

_____

_____

NOTES:

RECIPE TITLE: _____

MAKES _____ PIZZA(S)

INGREDIENTS

DOUGH: _____   _____
_____   _____
_____   _____
_____   _____

SAUCE: _____   _____
_____   _____
_____   _____
_____   _____

TOPPINGS: _____   _____
_____   _____
_____   _____

DIRECTIONS

_____
_____
_____
_____
_____
_____
_____
_____
_____

NOTES:

FAVORITE PIZZA RECIPES

RECIPE TITLE: _____

MAKES _____ PIZZA(S)

INGREDIENTS

DOUGH: _____   _____
_____   _____
_____   _____

SAUCE: _____   _____
_____   _____
_____   _____
_____   _____

TOPPINGS: _____   _____
_____   _____
_____   _____

DIRECTIONS

_____
_____
_____
_____
_____
_____
_____
_____
_____
_____

NOTES:

RECIPE TITLE: _____

MAKES _____ PIZZA(S)

INGREDIENTS

DOUGH: _____   _____

_____   _____

_____   _____

SAUCE: _____   _____

_____   _____

_____   _____

_____   _____

TOPPINGS: _____   _____

_____   _____

_____   _____

DIRECTIONS

_____

_____

_____

_____

_____

_____

_____

_____

NOTES:

Chapter Four

BAKING METHODS

FOR "REGULAR" ROUND-STYLE PIZZA

There are many different ways to bake pizza, and in this chapter, you'll learn the most common methods: in the home oven on a pizza pan, cast iron skillet, or baking stone/ steel; in an outdoor pizza oven; and on a propane or charcoal grill. If all you need is a handy reference chart of oven temperatures and baking/cooking times, flip to page 126. If you want to make pizza using a specific pan or baking surface, skip ahead to that page and study up. Then, use the notebook spreads at the end of the chapter to create planning schedules and record actual temperatures and baking/cooking times for the methods you explore.

Need baking instructions for other pizza styles? Flip to the pages below:

THIN-CRUST   page 59

GLUTEN-FREE   page 64

SICILIAN (RECTANGULAR SLAB-STYLE)   page 66

DETROIT-STYLE   page 176

GRANDMA-STYLE   page 174

 **QUICK-REFERENCE CHART** / PREP/COOK TIMES FOR DIFFERENT METHODS

BAKING METHOD	OVEN TEMPERATURE	HEAT-UP/ PREP TIME	BAKE/COOK TIME
PIZZA PAN OR BAKING SHEET	500°F	30 minutes	10 to 15 minutes
BAKING STONE OR STEEL PLATE	550°F, then Broil	1 hour	6 to 8 minutes
CAST IRON SKILLET OR PIZZA PAN	500°F	45 minutes	5 minutes on the stove, 10 minutes in the oven
OUTDOOR PIZZA OVEN	700°F to 1,000°F	Depends on the model	1 to 3 minutes
OUTDOOR GRILL	400 to 500°F	Depends on the type of grill	5 to 8 minutes

HOW TO MAKE PIZZA ON A PIZZA PAN OR BAKING SHEET

This is the simplest, least fussy way to make pizza, but there are two important things to keep in mind for best results. First, stretch or roll out the dough so it's thin and even all the way across and will therefore bake evenly. And second, bake the pizza until the underside has browned. If you take it out of the oven too early, the crust won't cook all the way through and you'll have soggy, gummy slices.

BEST DOUGH TO USE:
Any "regular" round-style dough (if you use 1-Hour Dough, 100% Whole Wheat Dough, or another denser recipe, roll it out so it's thin enough to cook all the way through)

EQUIPMENT:
12 to 14 inch round dark colored metal pizza pan or heavy-duty rimmed baking sheet

1. **GET THE OVEN READY.** Set a rack in the middle position and preheat the oven to 500°F. Let the oven heat up for about 30 minutes.

2. **TOP THE DOUGH.** Stretch or roll out a ball of pizza dough, place it on a dark metal pizza pan or heavy-duty rimmed baking sheet, and add toppings.

3. **BAKE THE PIZZA.** Put the pan in the oven and bake for 10 to 15 minutes, rotating the pan about halfway into baking, until the edges of the crust are golden and the underside is evenly browned all the way across.

4. **TAKE THE PIZZA OUT OF THE OVEN.** Remove the pan from the oven and slide the hot pizza onto a large cutting board. Wait a few minutes, add garnishes, then slice and serve.

HOW TO MAKE PIZZA ON A BAKING STONE OR STEEL

For the crispiest, char-spotted crusts, you'll need to create a super-hot baking environment with a stone or steel. The only downsides: These slabs are heavy and cumbersome and require a pizza peel, which takes practice to master.

BEST DOUGH TO USE:
Any "regular" round-style dough

EQUIPMENT:
Baking stone or steel plate (see page 19)

Pizza peel (see page 19) or upside-down baking sheet

Long offset spatula

1. **PUT THE STONE OR STEEL IN THE OVEN.** If you're using a baking stone, place it on a rack in the top third of the oven. If you're using a steel plate, place it on a rack in the bottom third of the oven.

2. **GET THE OVEN READY.** Preheat the oven to 550°F or as high as it will go. Let the oven heat up for 45 minutes to 1 hour, then switch the setting to Broil on high (only if your broiler is in the top of the oven).

3. **TOP THE DOUGH ON A PIZZA PEEL.** Stretch or roll out a ball of pizza dough, place it on a floured peel or upside-down baking sheet, and add toppings. Slip a long offset spatula between the dough and peel all the way around, then jerk the peel forward and back a few times to make sure the dough will launch.

4. **TRANSFER THE TOPPED DOUGH ONTO THE HOT STONE/STEEL.** Open the oven door and quickly shimmy the topped dough from the peel onto the hot steel or stone. Bake, rotating the pizza every minute or two, until the crust is golden around the edges and evenly browned on the bottom. This could take anywhere from 6 to 8 minutes, depending on your oven.

5. **TAKE THE PIZZA OUT OF THE OVEN.** Slip the peel under the pizza and remove it from the oven. Transfer the hot pizza to a large cutting board, wait a few minutes, then add garnishes, slice, and serve.

VIDEO DEMO: USING A PIZZA PEEL

A CASE FOR TWO PIZZA PEELS:
If you have the space, I highly recommend getting one wood, bamboo, or composite peel for launching and another perforated metal peel for turning and retrieving. Raw dough sticks less to wooden, bamboo, and composite peels, making these ideal for topping dough and shimmying it onto the hot stone or steel in the oven, and the thin, perforated metal peel slips easily under the pizza as it bakes, allowing excess flour to drop through it as you rotate the pizza and then take it out of the oven.

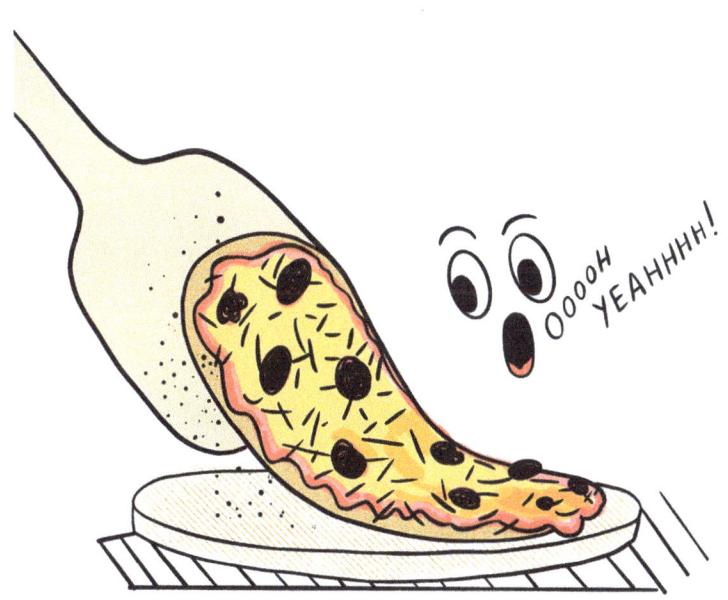

HOW TO MAKE PIZZA IN A CAST-IRON PIZZA PAN OR SKILLET

Want a crispy crust, but don't feel like investing in a bulky stone or steel? Cast iron skillets and pizza pans are great middle grounds between pizza pans and baking stones/steels. Just remember to use oven mitts!

BEST DOUGH TO USE:
Any "regular" round-style dough (if you use 1-Hour Dough, 100% Whole Wheat Dough, or another denser recipe, roll it out so it's thin enough to cook all the way through)

EQUIPMENT:
12-inch cast iron skillet or 12- to 14-inch cast iron pizza pan

Thick potholders

2 wooden spatulas

1. **GET THE OVEN READY.** Set a rack in the middle position and preheat the oven to 500°F for 30 to 45 minutes.

2. **PREP THE DOUGH.** Roll or stretch a ball of pizza dough into a circle that's just a little wider than the skillet or pan you are using.

3. **PREHEAT THE SKILLET ON THE STOVE.** Put your cast-iron skillet or pizza pan on the stove over medium heat for 3 to 5 minutes, until it's very hot.

4. **PAR-COOK THE DOUGH.** Add 1 tablespoon of olive oil and tilt the skillet or pan to coat the bottom. (You may need to use up to 2 tablespoons of oil if your pan/skillet is 14-inches or wider in diameter.) Lay the rolled- or stretched-out dough in the skillet and pat it out evenly. Cook for 2 to 3 minutes, just until the dough bubbles and is light golden brown on the underside. Turn off the stove.

5. **TOP AND BAKE.** Quickly add sauce, toppings, and cheese, then transfer the skillet/pan to the oven. Bake for 10 to 12 minutes, until the cheese melts and begins to brown.

6. **FINISH AND SERVE.** Remove the skillet/pan from the oven and use two spatulas to transfer the pizza to a cutting board. Let it cool for a few minutes, add garnishes, then slice and serve.

> **NOTE:** If you only have a 10-inch cast iron skillet, use half of a 14- to 16-ounce dough ball for each pizza.

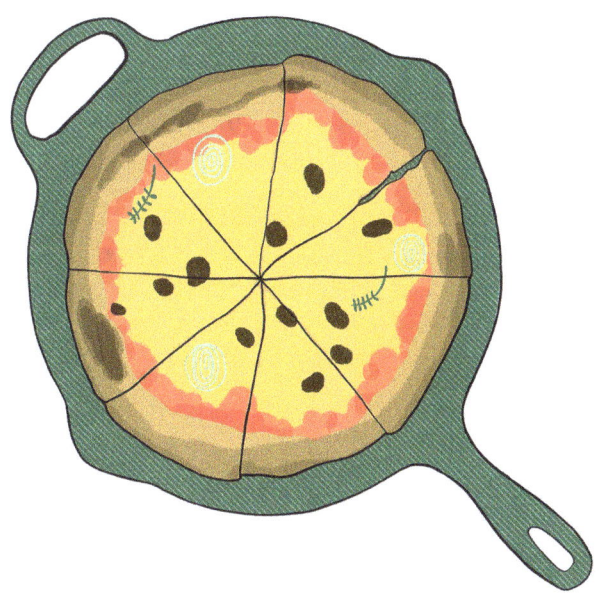

HOW TO MAKE PIZZA IN A PIZZA OVEN

Your pizza oven likely came with an instruction manual, but just in case it didn't, here are general directions that should work with any model.

BEST DOUGH TO USE:
Neapolitan (page 56)

New York–Style (page 54)

EQUIPMENT:
Propane, wood-fired, or electric pizza oven

Infrared thermometer

Metal pizza peel, preferably perforated

Metal turning peel

Fire-proof gloves

Offset spatula

1. **PREP THE TOPPINGS.** Make sure your ball of dough is at room temperature. Mix the sauce, slice veggies, grate or dice cheese, and place all other toppings in prep bowls on table or work surface close to the pizza oven.

2. **FIRE UP THE OVEN.** Light your pizza oven according to the manufacturer's directions.

3. **TEST THE TEMPERATURE.** Let the pizza oven heat up until the stone measures somewhere between 700°F and 1,000°F on an infrared thermometer (this could take anywhere from 15 to 30 minutes, depending on the model and type of oven).

4. **STRETCH OUT AND TOP YOUR PIZZA DOUGH.** Once the oven reaches the desired temperature, stretch or roll out a ball of dough to a 12- to 14-inch round. If your dough is too thick, it will burn on the outside before it cooks all the way through, so make sure you stretch or roll it out as evenly as possible; it should be thin enough to see light through it. Place the dough on a lightly floured pizza peel and add sauce, cheese, and other toppings, shimmying the peel periodically to make sure the dough doesn't stick.

5. **TRANSFER THE TOPPED DOUGH TO THE OVEN.** If the dough doesn't slide around when you jerk the peel back and forth, dust a long offset spatula with flour and slide it back and forth between the dough and the peel until the dough moves freely. Put on fire-proof gloves, open the oven door, and bring the peel to the oven. Use a quick, forward-and-back jerking motion to slide the topped dough from the peel onto the hot baking surface.

6. **BAKE UNTIL THE CRUST IS EVENLY BROWNED.** Cook the pizza, rotating it every 10 to 20 seconds, until it's evenly browned on the bottom and charred in spots on top and around the edges (this could take anywhere from 1 to 6 minutes, depending on the oven you're using). If you have a smaller, circular turning peel, use that to rotate the pizza during baking. If you don't have a turning peel, quickly take the pizza out of the oven with your regular peel, rotate it by hand, and then return it to the oven.

7. **TAKE THE PIZZA OUT OF THE OVEN.** Carefully slide your peel under the pizza and retrieve it from the oven. Let it rest on a cutting board for a few minutes, add garnishes, then slice and serve.

HOW TO MAKE PIZZA ON THE GRILL

Pizza dough loves heat and wood-fired ovens—so, naturally, it's also a great fit for grilling. The main differences, though, are that the dough is grilled on one side before topping, and it cooks from the bottom up, meaning raw vegetable toppings won't get as tender as they would in a pizza oven or home oven.

BEST DOUGH TO USE:
Any "regular" round-style dough

EQUIPMENT:
Propane or charcoal grill

Parchment paper

Pastry brush and small ramekin

Tongs

2 spatulas or a pizza peel

1. **PREP THE TOPPINGS.** Make sure your ball of dough is at room temperature. Mix the sauce, slice veggies, grate or dice cheese, and place all other toppings in prep bowls on a table or work surface close to the grill. Fill a small ramekin with grapeseed oil or vegetable/canola oil and grab a pastry brush.

2. **GET THE GRILL READY.** Scrape the grill grates to make sure they're clean. Turn your propane grill to medium-high or light your charcoal grill for direct heat. Let the grill heat up until it reaches a temperature between 400 and 500°F. If your grill doesn't have a built-in thermometer, use the hand test: If you can hold your hand a few inches above the grate for 5 to 7 seconds without burning yourself, you've reached medium-high.

3. **STRETCH OR ROLL OUT THE DOUGH.** Stretch or roll out the dough to a 12- to 14-inch round or oval. Place the dough on a piece of parchment paper. Use the pastry brush to coat the top of the dough with grapeseed or vegetable oil, making sure it is lightly coated all the way to the edges.

4. **GRILL THE FIRST SIDE.** Flip the dough onto the grill, oiled side down, and peel off the parchment paper. Close the grill and cook for 2 to 3 minutes, just until you see deep brown grill marks on the bottom.

5. **FLIP AND TOP.** Using tongs, grab the crust off the grill and flip it onto a plate so the grill marks are facing up. Add sauce, toppings, and cheese.

6. **GRILL THE OTHER SIDE.** Reduce the heat slightly, open the grill, and oil the grates with grapeseed or vegetable/canola oil. Use two spatulas or a pizza peel to transfer the topped crust to the grill grates. Close the lid and grill for another 3 to 5 minutes, until the cheese is melted and there are brown grill marks on the bottom.

7. **TAKE THE PIZZA OFF THE GRILL.** Use the spatulas or pizza peel to transfer the pizza from the grill to a cutting board. Garnish, slice, and serve.

NOTE: Go easy on toppings! Since grilled pizzas cook from the bottom up, the toppings won't get tender and caramelized like they do in a pizza oven or home oven. For best results, spread on some sauce, top it with a handful of thinly sliced veggies or meats, and sprinkle with ¾ to 1 cup of shredded or diced cheese.

SCHEDULES / FOR DIFFERENT BAKING METHODS

Use the following charts to help you plan for pizza night, based on your preferred baking method(s) and when you want to eat.

TARGET PIZZA NIGHT DINNERTIME: _____

DOUGH RECIPE: _____ (PAGE _____)

BAKING METHOD: _____

DATE/TIME	STEP	NOTES
	Mix the ingredients	
	Start first proof	
	Start second proof (if applicable)	
	Preheat the oven/ start final rest time	
	Stretch or roll out the dough	
	Top and bake	

TARGET PIZZA NIGHT DINNERTIME: _____

DOUGH RECIPE: _____ (PAGE _____)

BAKING METHOD: _____

DATE/TIME	STEP	NOTES
	Mix the ingredients	
	Start first proof	
	Start second proof (if applicable)	
	Preheat the oven/ start final rest time	
	Stretch or roll out the dough	
	Top and bake	

TARGET PIZZA NIGHT DINNERTIME: _____

DOUGH RECIPE: _____ (PAGE _____)

BAKING METHOD: _____

DATE/TIME	STEP	NOTES
	Mix the ingredients	
	Start first proof	
	Start second proof (if applicable)	
	Preheat the oven/ start final rest time	
	Stretch or roll out the dough	
	Top and bake	

TARGET PIZZA NIGHT DINNERTIME: _____

DOUGH RECIPE: _____ (PAGE _____)

BAKING METHOD: _____

DATE/TIME	STEP	NOTES
	Mix the ingredients	
	Start first proof	
	Start second proof (if applicable)	
	Preheat the oven/ start final rest time	
	Stretch or roll out the dough	
	Top and bake	

TARGET PIZZA NIGHT DINNERTIME: _____

DOUGH RECIPE: _____ (PAGE _____)

BAKING METHOD: _____

DATE/TIME	STEP	NOTES
	Mix the ingredients	
	Start first proof	
	Start second proof (if applicable)	
	Preheat the oven/ start final rest time	
	Stretch or roll out the dough	
	Top and bake	

TARGET PIZZA NIGHT DINNERTIME: _____

DOUGH RECIPE: _____ (PAGE _____)

BAKING METHOD:

DATE/TIME	STEP	NOTES
	Mix the ingredients	
	Start first proof	
	Start second proof (if applicable)	
	Preheat the oven/ start final rest time	
	Stretch or roll out the dough	
	Top and bake	

TARGET PIZZA NIGHT DINNERTIME: _____

DOUGH RECIPE: _____ (PAGE _____)

BAKING METHOD: _____

DATE/TIME	STEP	NOTES
	Mix the ingredients	
	Start first proof	
	Start second proof (if applicable)	
	Preheat the oven/ start final rest time	
	Stretch or roll out the dough	
	Top and bake	

BAKING LOG

DATE	PIZZA BAKING METHOD	OVEN/COOKING TEMP.	ACTUAL BAKING/ COOKING TIME	NOTES

DATE	PIZZA BAKING METHOD	OVEN/COOKING TEMP.	ACTUAL BAKING/ COOKING TIME	NOTES

BAKING LOG

DATE	PIZZA BAKING METHOD	OVEN/COOKING TEMP.	ACTUAL BAKING/ COOKING TIME	NOTES

DATE	PIZZA BAKING METHOD	OVEN/COOKING TEMP.	ACTUAL BAKING/ COOKING TIME	NOTES

Chapter Five

MAKING IT A MEAL

Pizza's great on its own, but there are certain pairings that take it to the next level. For example, green salad and ice-cold pilsner or lemonade can help balance the richness of Detroit-style meat lover's pizza, and an appetizer spread of creamy dips, chips, and antipasti can make simple Margherita feel more like a meal. Another favorite: veggie supreme pizza with quinoa salad, followed by brownies and ice cream.

In this chapter, you'll find inspiration for any kind of menu—from easy weeknight meals to low-key hangouts and big celebrations—including starters, side dishes, desserts, and beverages that go especially well with pizza. Use it as a reference to plan your next pizza night or party, then flip to the guided notebook pages to sketch out the menu.

WHAT TO SERVE WITH PIZZA

APPETIZERS

ANTIPASTI—A grazing board of marinated olives, cheeses, cured meats, cherry peppers, roasted red peppers, jarred artichoke hearts, pickles, nuts, cherry tomatoes, and crackers

BRUSCHETTA—Thin, toasted bread slices rubbed with garlic and topped with marinated diced tomatoes and onion, fresh basil, and a drizzle of balsamic glaze

CHICKEN WINGS—Seasoned and baked/roasted chicken wings, glazed with Buffalo or barbecue sauce if desired and served with ranch or blue cheese dressing

COCKTAIL WEENIES, MEATBALLS, OR SAUSAGE BITES—Bite-sized sausages, meatballs, or mini hot dogs to satisfy the meat eaters (especially if your pizzas are vegetarian)

CRUDITÉS—Raw vegetables like carrots, celery, bell peppers, sugar snap or snow peas, radishes, cucumber, broccoli, and green beans served with bagna cauda (a sauce made of olive oil, butter, garlic, and anchovies), creamy dip, or on their own

DIP—Tapenade, muhammara, hummus, beet pesto, green goddess, ranch; serve with chips, crackers, and/or raw veggies before the meal, then keep leftovers on the table for dunking crusts

PROSCIUTTO- OR BACON-WRAPPED FIGS OR DATES — Cut fresh figs in half, top with a dollop of whipped herbed goat cheese, and wrap them in strips of prosciutto; stuff pitted dates with goat cheese or blue cheese, wrap them in thin strips of bacon, and bake until crispy

STUFFED MUSHROOMS — Cremini caps filled with sautéed mushroom stems, garlic, shallot, herbs, and breadcrumbs and baked until the caps are tender and the stuffing is nice and crispy on top

SIDE DISHES

BEANS — Steamed fresh or frozen edamame, chickpea salad, three-bean salad, warmed canned beans tossed with pesto

CAPRESE — Sliced tomato and fresh mozzarella topped with basil leaves and seasoned with salt, pepper, olive oil, and balsamic glaze

COOKED VEGETABLES — Steamed broccoli, peas, corn on the cob, green beans, or asparagus; sautéed mushrooms or broccoli rabe; roasted beets, carrots, butternut squash, or Brussels sprouts; grilled eggplant, bell peppers, shishito peppers, or zucchini

GRAIN AND VEGGIE SALAD — Tabbouleh (bulgur with fresh herbs) or quinoa or wheat berries with spring mix, raw or cooked veggies, and vinaigrette

GREEN SALAD — Caesar, chopped salad, arugula with shaved parm, massaged kale and dried fruit, citrus and fennel, baby spinach; if your pizza has extra cheese or rich toppings like bacon, add radishes, pickled vegetables, or vinaigrette to your salad to create balance.

RATATOUILLE — A stew-like dish or casserole of simmered or baked eggplant, tomato, onion, bell pepper, zucchini, garlic, and herbs

SAUTÉED GREENS — Kale, collard greens, mustard greens, Swiss chard, bok choy, escarole, and spinach, wilted in a pan with olive oil, maybe a little garlic or squeeze of lemon, and pinches of salt and pepper

SLAW — Raw shredded or julienned cabbage, apple, carrots, fennel, broccoli, celery root, and/or kohlrabi tossed with a tangy-sweet dressing of mayonnaise, mustard, sugar, vinegar, and celery seeds

SOUP — Lighter, refreshing recipes like minestrone, blended tomato soup (especially if you're serving white pizza), cream of cauliflower, kale and white bean, or any vegetable soup with pesto or herbs

DESSERTS

BAKED OR POACHED FRUIT — Simple cooked whole fruits, like apples, pears, peaches, apricots, or nectarines, served with vanilla ice cream and/or whipped cream

BERRY CRISP — Fresh or frozen berries baked with a crispy oat-and-brown-sugar topping

COOKIES OR BARS — Smaller bites or squares of decadent chocolate chip cookies, brownies/blondies, fruit bars, rice cereal treats

FRESH FRUIT — A salad of chopped seasonal fruits or a finely chopped salsa served with cinnamon-sugar chips

PARFAIT — Larger or individual desserts made by alternating layers of ice cream, yogurt, or pudding; chopped fresh fruit or berries; and crunchy granola, crushed cookies, or cake

GRANITA, SORBET, OR ICE CREAM — Frozen treats with flavors that balance your pizza recipes. For example, if the pizza's rich with cheese and meats, serve granita or fruit sorbet to lighten things up; if you opted for minimal vegetarian pizza toppings, add some luxury to the meal with chocolate ice cream or gelato.

DRINKS

ALCOHOL-FREE — Agua fresca (fresh fruit blended with water, citrus juice, and a little sweetener), flavored seltzer, ice water with lemon or lime wedges, iced tea, lemonade, soda

WINE — Sparkling or regular rosé for white pizza; bold, fruity red (sangiovese, malbec, cabernet sauvignon) for pepperoni or meat lover's pizza; Chianti, pinot noir, or dry rosé for plain cheese pizza or margherita; light, chilled red (like Lambrusco) or full-bodied white wine (like chardonnay) for veggie pizzas; riesling for fruity pizzas like Hawaiian; light and bubbly wines (prosecco, Lambrusco, sparkling rosé) for a variety of different toppings

BEER — Kolsch or Belgian Tripel for white pizza; pilsner, amber ale, lager, brown ale, or IPA for pepperoni or meat lover's pizza; pale ale, blonde, or lager for plain cheese pizza or margherita; wheat beer, saison, or Kolsch for veggie pizzas; golden ale, smoked beer, or brown ale for fruity pizzas like Hawaiian; IPA or pilsner for a variety of different toppings

FAVORITE PIZZA NIGHT MENUS

DATE: ___ / ___ / ___

OCCASION:

GUESTS:

Appetizer(s)

Sides(s)

PIZZA(S)

DRINK(S):

Dessert

NOTES:

FAVORITE PIZZA NIGHT MENUS

DATE: ___ / ___ / ___

OCCASION:

GUESTS:

_____
_____
_____
_____
_____
_____
_____
_____
_____
_____
_____
_____
_____
_____
_____

Appetizer(s)

Sides(s)

PIZZA(S)

DRINK(S):

Dessert

NOTES:

FAVORITE PIZZA NIGHT MENUS

DATE: ___ /___ /___

OCCASION:

GUESTS:

Appetizer(s)

Sides(s)

PIZZA(S)

DRINK(S):

Dessert

NOTES:

FAVORITE PIZZA NIGHT MENUS

DATE: ___ / ___ / ___

OCCASION:

GUESTS:

_____

_____

_____

_____

_____

_____

_____

_____

_____

_____

_____

_____

_____

_____

_____

_____

_____

Appetizer(s)

Sides(s)

PIZZA(S)

DRINK(S):

Dessert

NOTES:

Chapter Six

COMPOSED PIZZA RECIPES

"Learn the rules like a pro,
so you can break them
like an artist."

Pablo Picasso

In this chapter, you'll find 10 recipes
to hone your skills and inspire your inner
pizzaiolo. There's the O.G., Margherita,
with its Neapolitan dough and holy trinity
of tomato sauce, mozzarella, and basil. Then,
the pizzeria stalwarts — "Plain" Cheese,
Veggie Supreme, Meat Lover's, and Garlicky
White — all classics for good reason.
From there, up the ante with intermediate
techniques, like the deconstructed white
sauce in Bacon, Leek, and Cream and paper-
thin sliced spuds in Roman Potato Pizza
(which happens to be vegan-friendly, by the
way). And, finally, expand your horizons with
slabs of focaccia-esque Grandma-style with
vegetables, Detroit-style with pepperoni,
and Philly-style Tomato Pie (Go Birds!).

Follow each recipe at least once, then experiment with different doughs, topping combinations, garnishes, and condiments.

MARGHERITA PIZZA

100% traditional pizza Margherita is made with only Neapolitan-Style Dough (using 00 flour), crushed San Marzano tomatoes, buffalo mozzarella, high-quality extra-virgin olive oil, and fresh Italian basil leaves. However, if you don't have time for the long fermentation, Beer Dough (page 50), Overnight Dough (page 53), Sourdough Starter Dough (page 51), or any other recipe from the "Regular" Round-Style Dough category will also work great.

MAKES 1
(12- TO 14-INCH)
PIZZA

1 ball Neapolitan (page 56) or other "regular" round-style pizza dough (at room temperature)

½ to ⅔ cup No-Cook Marinara Sauce (page 84)

4 ounces fresh mozzarella, cut into ½-inch cubes

Extra-virgin olive oil

Kosher salt and freshly ground black pepper

4 to 6 large Italian basil leaves

If you're using a steel plate, place it in the bottom third of the oven. If you're using a baking stone, place it in the top third of the oven. If you're using a baking sheet or pizza pan, set an oven rack in the center position. Preheat the oven to 500°F (if using a baking sheet) or as high as it will go (if using a baking stone/steel). Let the oven preheat for 30 to 45 minutes. Then, if you're using a baking stone/steel, change the setting to Broil on high and let it heat up for another 10 minutes or so.

Stretch or roll out your dough to a 12- to 14-inch round and transfer it to a baking sheet or lightly floured pizza peel (if using a baking stone/steel). Prick all but the edges of the dough with a fork to prevent large bubbles from forming in the oven.

Pour a tablespoon or two of olive oil into a small ramekin. Use your fingertip or a pastry brush to coat the edges of the dough, being careful not to let the oil drip down the sides (this will make it difficult to launch if using a pizza peel). Spread the sauce evenly over the dough, leaving a ½-inch border all around. Add the mozzarella, drizzle lightly with olive oil, and season with a pinch of salt and a few grinds of black pepper.

Bake, rotating the pizza every couple of minutes if using a steel plate or baking stone, until the cheese has charred in spots, the crust is golden around the edges, and the underside is evenly browned — 10 to 15 minutes on the baking sheet, 6 to 8 minutes on the baking stone/steel. Remove the pizza from the oven.

Tear the fresh basil leaves into small pieces and scatter them on top of the pizza. Drizzle lightly with olive oil and let cool for a few minutes. Slice and serve.

CLASSIC CHEESE PIZZA (TOPPINGS OPTIONAL)

If round, thin(ish) pizzas are your jam, then this is the recipe you've been looking for. Keep it "plain" with red sauce, mozzarella, and finely shredded parm; add a cup of thin-sliced pepperoni; or experiment with seasonal (or leftover) vegetables.

MAKES 1
(12- TO 14-INCH)
PIZZA

1 ball "regular" round-style pizza dough (at room temperature)

Extra-virgin olive oil

½ to ⅔ cup No-Cook Marinara (page 84), Slow-Simmered Pizza Sauce (page 85), or jarred/canned pizza sauce

4 to 6 ounces low-moisture mozzarella, shredded, or fresh mozzarella, cut into ½-inch dice (1 to 1½ cups)

1 to 2 cups additional toppings (sliced or chopped olives, thinly sliced pepperoni, vegetables, etc.), optional — see Topping Tip

2 tablespoons to ¼ cup finely shredded or grated sharp/aged cheese (like parmesan, extra-sharp cheddar, or aged gouda)

Kosher salt

Freshly ground black pepper

Chopped fresh basil, mint, oregano, or chives, for garnish (optional)

NOTES:

If you're using a steel plate, place it in the bottom third of the oven. If you're using a baking stone, place it in the top third of the oven. If you're using a baking sheet or pizza pan, set an oven rack in the center position. Preheat the oven to 500°F (if using a baking sheet) or as high as it will go (if using a baking stone/steel). Let the oven preheat for 30 to 45 minutes. Then, if you're using a baking stone/steel, change the setting to Broil on high and let it heat up for another 10 minutes or so.

Stretch or roll out your dough to a 12- to 14-inch round and transfer it to a baking sheet or lightly floured pizza peel (if using a baking stone/steel). Prick all but the edges of the dough with a fork to prevent large bubbles from forming in the oven.

Pour a tablespoon or two of olive oil into a small ramekin. Use your fingertip or a pastry brush to coat the edges of the dough, being careful not to let the oil drip down the sides (this will make it difficult to launch if using a pizza peel). Spread the sauce evenly over the dough, leaving a ½-inch border all around. Add the mozzarella and any other toppings, and finish with the finely shredded sharp cheese. Season with a pinch of salt and a few grinds of black pepper.

Bake, rotating the pizza every couple of minutes if using a steel plate or baking stone, until the cheese has charred in spots, the crust is golden around the edges, and the underside is evenly browned — 10 to 15 minutes on the baking sheet, 6 to 8 minutes on the baking stone/steel. Remove the pizza from the oven.

Sprinkle on the chopped fresh herbs, if using, and season with a drizzle of olive oil, a pinch of salt, and a few grinds of black pepper, if desired. Let cool for a few minutes, then slice and serve.

TOPPING TIP: If you plan to use high-moisture toppings, such as raw vegetables, limit them to no more than 1 cup for a 12-inch and 1½ cups for a 14-inch pizza. Unless they are pre-cooked, ingredients like mushrooms, bell peppers, tomatoes, and zucchini will emit water as they bake; if there's no room for that water to evaporate, you'll end up with a soupy, soggy mess.

VEGGIE SUPREME PIZZA

Never sure how many vegetables you need for homemade pizza? Consider this recipe a template for future experimentation. Here, I've found an ideal balance of fresh herbs, red onion, mushrooms, green pepper, olives, and chopped tomato. Make it as written, then play with different ingredients and combinations, keeping moisture content in mind (see the Topping Tip on page 163).

MAKES 1
(12- TO 14-INCH)
PIZZA

1 ball "regular" round-style pizza dough (at room temperature)

½ cup No-Cook Marinara (page 84), Slow-Simmered Pizza Sauce (page 85), or jarred/canned pizza sauce

2 tablespoons finely chopped fresh basil and oregano (half and half, or all basil)

4 ounces low-moisture mozzarella cheese, shredded (1 cup)

¼ medium red onion, thinly sliced

3 medium cremini mushrooms, stemmed and thinly sliced

½ small green bell pepper, stemmed, seeded, and thinly sliced

¼ cup sliced black olives

½ medium Roma (or similar) tomato, seeded and chopped

Kosher salt

Freshly ground black pepper

NOTES:

If you're using a steel plate, place it in the bottom third of the oven. If you're using a baking stone, place it in the top third of the oven. If you're using a baking sheet or pizza pan, set an oven rack in the center position. Preheat the oven to 500°F (if using a baking sheet) or as high as it will go (if using a baking stone/steel). Let the oven preheat for 30 to 45 minutes. Then, if you're using a baking stone/steel, change the setting to Broil on high and let it heat up for another 10 minutes or so.

Stretch or roll out your dough to a 12- to 14-inch round and transfer it to a baking sheet or lightly floured pizza peel (if using a baking stone/steel). Prick all but the edges of the dough with a fork to prevent large bubbles from forming in the oven.

Spread the sauce on the dough, leaving a ½-inch border all around, then sprinkle with the chopped fresh herbs and half of the cheese. Add the remaining toppings in this order: onion, mushrooms, bell pepper, olives, remaining cheese, and tomato. Season with a pinch of salt and a few grinds of black pepper.

Bake, rotating the pizza every couple of minutes if using a steel plate or baking stone, until the crust is golden around the edges and the underside is evenly browned — 10 to 15 minutes on the baking sheet, 6 to 8 minutes on the baking stone/steel.

Remove the pizza from the oven and let it rest for a couple minutes, then slice and serve.

MEAT LOVER'S PIZZA

How many different meat toppings do you need to achieve "meat lover's" status? I use five in my version (ground beef, Italian sausage, bacon, ham, and pepperoni), but some pizzerias stick to as little as three or as many as seven. The trick, as usual, is balance. If you add more, reduce the amounts of everything; if you cut one or two, use a little more of the remaining ones.

**MAKES 1
(12- TO 14-INCH)
PIZZA**

¼ pound 90% lean ground beef

1 link mild or hot Italian sausage, casing removed

2 slices bacon, chopped

1 ball "regular" round-style pizza dough (at room temperature)

½ cup No-Cook Marinara (page 84), Slow-Simmered Pizza Sauce (page 85), or jarred/canned pizza sauce

1 shallot, very thinly sliced

4 to 6 ounces low-moisture mozzarella, shredded (1 to 1½ cups)

¼ cup diced deli ham or ham steak

1 (2-inch) piece pepperoni, thinly sliced (⅓ cup)

Red pepper flakes (optional)

¼ cup finely shredded parmesan or pecorino cheese

1 to 2 tablespoons chopped fresh parsley and/or chives

NOTES:

If you're using a steel plate, place it in the bottom third of the oven. If you're using a baking stone, place it in the top third of the oven. If you're using a baking sheet or pizza pan, set an oven rack in the center position. Preheat the oven to 500°F (if using a baking sheet) or as high as it will go (if using a baking stone/steel). Let the oven preheat for 30 to 45 minutes. Then, if you're using a baking stone/steel, change the setting to Broil on high and let it heat up for another 10 minutes or so.

Place a skillet over medium-high heat and add the ground beef and sausage. Cook, breaking up the meat with a wooden spatula, just until it's no longer pink, about 5 minutes. Scrape the cooked meat onto a plate, leaving the grease in the skillet. Return the pan to medium-high heat and add the chopped bacon. Cook, stirring, just until the pieces begin to brown around the edges, 3 to 5 minutes. Turn off the heat, transfer the bacon to the plate with the ground meat, and pour the grease from the skillet into a small heatproof ramekin. Blot the meat with a paper towel if it looks too greasy for your taste.

Stretch or roll out your dough to a 12- to 14-inch round and transfer it to a baking sheet or lightly floured pizza peel (if using a baking stone/steel). Prick all but the edges of the dough with a fork to prevent large bubbles from forming in the oven.

Brush the edges of the dough with some of the grease from cooking the meat. Add the sauce and spread it evenly, leaving a ½-inch border all around, then arrange the thinly sliced shallot or onion on top of the sauce, followed by half of the mozzarella cheese. Add the cooked meats, bacon, ham, and pepperoni, a pinch or two of pepper flakes (if desired), the remaining mozzarella, and the parmesan.

Bake, rotating the pizza every couple of minutes if using a steel plate or baking stone, until the crust is golden around the edges the underside is evenly browned — 10 to 15 minutes on the baking sheet, 6 to 8 minutes on the baking stone/steel.

Take the pizza out of the oven and let it sit for a minute or two, then top with the chopped parsley and/or chives; slice and serve.

GARLICKY WHITE PIZZA

The best white pizzas are simple and elegant, topped with little more than creamy sauce and milky cheese. Add some roasted garlic, and you're on a whole new level of deliciousness.

MAKES 1
(12- TO 14-INCH)
PIZZA

FOR THE ROASTED GARLIC:

1 head garlic

1 tablespoon extra-virgin olive oil

FOR THE PIZZA:

Fine sea salt and freshly ground black pepper

Extra-virgin olive oil

1 ball "regular" pizza dough (at room temperature)

½ cup Ricotta Cream Sauce (page 86, made with chopped fresh basil and/or parsley)

4 ounces fresh mozzarella cheese, cut into ½-inch cubes (1 cup)

Pinch of crushed red chile flakes (optional)

1 tablespoon chopped fresh basil or parsley

NOTES:

SET UP THE OVEN: If you're using a steel plate, place it in the bottom third of the oven. If you're using a baking stone, place it in the top third of the oven. If you're using a baking sheet or pizza pan, set an oven rack in the center position.

TO ROAST THE GARLIC:

Preheat the oven to 400°F.

Rub most of the skin off of the garlic head, leaving just the thin layer that covers the cloves. Then, using a sharp knife, slice off the top ¼ to ½ inch of the garlic head, exposing the cloves. Place the garlic head on a square of aluminum foil, cut-side up, and drizzle the exposed garlic cloves with the olive oil. Fold the corners of the foil up and over the garlic head, then pinch the edges of foil together to make a sealed pouch.

Place the foil pouch on a baking sheet. Bake for 40 minutes or until the garlic cloves are very tender. (Check by carefully peeling back the foil and piercing a clove with the tip of a sharp knife; the knife should slide right in with very little resistance.)

Remove the garlic from the oven. Let it cool for a few minutes in the pouch, then carefully peel back the foil. When the head is cool enough to handle, hold it upside down over a ramekin and squeeze out the roasted cloves. Mash with a fork and set aside.

TO MAKE THE PIZZA:

Increase the oven temperature to 500°F (if using a baking sheet) or as high as it will go (if using a baking stone/steel). Let the oven heat up for 15 to 20 minutes. Then, if you're using a baking stone/steel, change the setting to Broil on high and let it heat up for another 10 minutes or so.

Stretch or roll out your dough to a 12- to 14-inch round and transfer it to a baking sheet or lightly floured pizza peel (if using a baking stone/steel). Prick all but the edges of the dough with a fork to prevent large bubbles from forming in the oven.

Spread the sauce evenly over the dough, leaving a ½-inch border all around. Top with the roasted garlic, distributing it as evenly as possible, then the mozzarella.

Bake, rotating the pizza every couple of minutes if using a steel plate or baking stone, until the cheese has charred in spots and the crust is golden around the edges and evenly browned on the underside — 10 to 15 minutes on the baking sheet, 6 to 8 minutes on the baking stone/steel.

Remove the pizza from the oven. Season with a pinch or two of salt and the dried chile flakes, if desired, sprinkle with the chopped basil or parsley, and drizzle with a little olive oil. Let cool for a few minutes, then slice and serve.

BACON, LEEK, AND CREAM PIZZA

Like the idea of white pizza, but want something less rich than ricotta cream? Here, the components are added separately— a thin coating of bacon grease, cheese, a drizzle of heavy cream—and merge together in the oven to create a fresh-tasting, creamy "sauce" that might just change your life.

MAKES 1
(12- TO 14-INCH)
PIZZA

½ pound thick-cut bacon, chopped

1 medium leek, trimmed, white and light green part halved lengthwise and sliced into thin half-moons

1 ball "regular" pizza dough (at room temperature)

4 ounces Gruyère, fontina, aged gouda, or sharp cheddar cheese, finely shredded (1 cup)

Kosher salt

Freshly ground black pepper

¼ cup heavy cream, divided

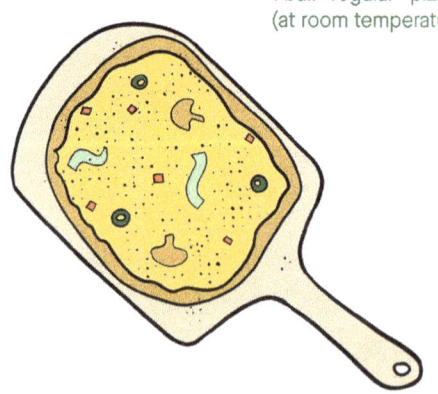

NOTES:

If you're using a steel plate, place it in the bottom third of the oven. If you're using a baking stone, place it in the top third of the oven. If you're using a baking sheet or pizza pan, set an oven rack in the center position. Preheat the oven to 500°F (if using a baking sheet) or as high as it will go (if using a baking stone/steel). Let the oven preheat for 30 to 45 minutes. Then, if you're using a baking stone/steel, change the setting to Broil on high and let it heat up for another 10 minutes or so.

In a medium skillet over medium heat, cook the bacon until it just begins to brown at the edges, 5 to 7 minutes. Remove the skillet from the heat and transfer the bacon to a paper towel–lined plate to drain. Pour the bacon grease into a small ramekin for brushing the dough.

While the bacon cooks, put the sliced leek in a colander and rinse it thoroughly under cold running water, using your fingertips to separate the layers. Drain well, transfer the leek slices to a paper towel–lined plate, and blot them dry with more paper towels.

Stretch or roll out your dough to a 12- to 14-inch round and transfer it to a baking sheet or lightly floured pizza peel (if using a baking stone/steel). Prick all but the edges of the dough with a fork to prevent large bubbles from forming in the oven.

Pour the heavy cream into a measuring cup or other spouted container. Use a pastry brush to spread a very thin layer of bacon grease all over the dough. Scatter the sliced leeks and cooked bacon on top, sprinkle with the cheese, and season with a pinch or two of salt and a few grinds of black pepper. Drizzle the toppings with half of the heavy cream.

Bake, rotating the pizza every couple of minutes if using a steel plate or baking stone, until the cheese has charred in spots and the crust is golden around the edges and evenly browned on the underside — 10 to 15 minutes on the baking sheet, 6 to 8 minutes on the baking stone/steel.

Remove the pizza from the oven and immediately drizzle the remaining heavy cream over top. Wait 3 to 5 minutes for the cream to congeal, then slice and serve.

TOPPING TIP: Make it vegetarian by skipping the bacon, using olive oil to brush the dough, and adding long, thinly sliced scallion "ribbons" and chopped fresh chives.

POTATO PIZZA WITH ROSEMARY AND OLIVE OIL

Based on an Italian classic, this pizza is topped with thinly sliced potatoes, olive oil, rosemary, and Parmigiano-Reggiano cheese. Leave off the cheese to make it vegan!

MAKES 1
(12- TO 14-INCH)
PIZZA

3 cups lukewarm water

1½ tablespoons kosher salt, plus more as needed

1 to 1½ pounds small to medium gold potatoes

2 tablespoons extra-virgin olive oil, plus more for drizzling

½ small yellow onion, minced (⅓ to ½ cup)

Freshly ground black pepper

2 tablespoons chopped fresh rosemary, divided

1 ball "regular" pizza dough (at room temperature)

3 tablespoons finely shredded Parmigiano-Reggiano cheese (optional)

Hot sauce, for serving (optional)

NOTES:

In a large bowl, whisk together the water and salt until the salt is completely dissolved.

Use a mandoline slicer or the slicing side of a box grater to slice the potatoes paper thin. Place the sliced potatoes in the bowl of salted water and press them down so they are fully submerged. Set aside to soak for 1 hour, then drain in a colander. (If you don't have time to soak the potatoes for an hour, blanch them instead: Measure 6 cups of water and 2 tablespoons kosher salt into a medium pot. Place the pot over high heat, bring the water to a boil, and add the sliced potatoes. Let the water come back to a boil, cook for 10 seconds, then immediately drain the potatoes.)

If you're using a baking stone or steel plate, place it in the center of the oven. If you're using a baking sheet or pizza pan, set an oven rack in the center position. Preheat the oven to 500°F.

Spread the soaked or blanched and drained potato slices on a paper towel–lined cutting board and pat them dry with extra paper towels.

Place the potato slices in a large bowl. Add the 2 tablespoons of olive oil, the minced onion, a few grinds of black pepper, a large pinch of salt, and 1 tablespoon of the chopped rosemary. Use your hands to gently toss everything together until the potatoes are evenly coated and the seasonings and onion are evenly distributed.

Stretch or roll out the pizza dough to a 12- to 14-inch round (or a 12-by-14-inch rectangle, for a classic Roman-style pizza). Transfer the dough to a baking sheet or lightly floured pizza peel (if using a baking stone/steel) and prick it all over with a fork to prevent big bubbles from forming in the oven.

Spread the potatoes in an even layer on top of the dough, making sure the potato slices go all the way to the edges of the dough. Sprinkle with another pinch or two of salt and a few grinds of black pepper.

Bake for 15 to 20 minutes, until the bottom of the crust is evenly browned and the potatoes are tender and beginning to brown in spots.

Remove the pizza from the oven. Drizzle with olive oil, season with a pinch of salt, and sprinkle the remaining tablespoon of chopped rosemary on top. Finish with the finely shredded Parmigiano-Reggiano cheese, if using. Slice and serve with hot sauce on the side, if using.

GRANDMA-STYLE PIZZA WITH ALL THE VEGGIES

Grandma Pizza is said to have originated on Long Island, New York, where Italian grandmothers whipped it up on the regular using Sicilian-style dough recipes they knew by heart and whatever toppings they had on hand. Think of this recipe as a template for making your own unique creations—it's a wonderful way to use up leftover produce at the end of the week.

MAKES 1
(13-BY-18-INCH)
PIZZA

1 recipe Sicilian Pan Pizza Dough (page 66)

2 tablespoons extra-virgin olive oil

10 ounces low-moisture mozzarella or other mild, semi-firm melting cheese, shredded (2½ cups)

1½ to 2 cups No-Cook Marinara (page 84), Slow-Simmered Pizza Sauce (page 85), or jarred/canned pizza sauce

2 to 2½ cups chopped or thinly sliced raw vegetables, such as mushrooms, bell peppers, olives, onion, and/or zucchini

⅓ cup finely grated parmesan, pecorino, aged gouda, or sharp cheddar cheese

Kosher salt and freshly ground black pepper

NOTES:

Follow the Sicilian Pan Pizza Dough recipe through step 3 and let it rise for 1 to 2 hours, until it about doubles in volume.

Preheat the oven to 500°F with a rack in the bottom position.

Grease a large (13-by-18-inch) dark-colored rimmed baking sheet with the olive oil. Place the dough in the pan and gently press it out with your fingertips until it fills the pan all the way to the edges. If it keeps shrinking back, let the dough rest for another 15 to 20 minutes and try again. After the dough is pressed out all the way to the corners, cover with plastic wrap or a clean kitchen towel and let the dough rest for 20 to 30 minutes.

When the dough is finished resting in the sheet pan, dimple it with your fingertips to prevent big bubbles from forming in the oven. Scatter all but ½ cup of the mozzarella evenly across the dough, spoon the sauce over top, and add the vegetables. Then, sprinkle with the remaining ½ cup of mozzarella and the Parmesan and season with a big pinch of salt and a few grinds of black pepper.

Bake for 15 minutes, turning once at the halfway mark, or until the underside of the crust is evenly browned. (Carefully lift up the pizza with an offset or other spatula to check for doneness.)

Remove the pizza from the oven, let cool for 5 minutes, then use two spatulas to transfer it to a large cutting board. Cut into squares and serve.

PREP TIP: To make it a quick weeknight meal, mix the dough and refrigerate it overnight, let it come to room temperature while you prep the toppings and preheat the oven, skip the extra proof time, and you'll have dinner on the table in less than an hour.

DETROIT-STYLE PEPPERONI PIZZA

Three characteristics make Detroit-style pizza stand out from its cousins, Sicilian-style pizza and grandma-style pizza: It's baked in a rectangular steel pan (just like the ones used to hold small parts in factories or catch oil drips in automotive shops); the cheese is scattered on all the way to the edges so it creates a crispy, caramelized crust; and the sauce goes on top, usually in long, thick lines.

MAKES 1
(9-BY-13-INCH)
PIZZA

1 recipe Sicilian Pan Pizza Dough (page 66)

1½ tablespoons extra-virgin olive oil

6 to 8 ounces pepperoni, thinly sliced (1 to 1½ cups)

8 ounces mild, semi-firm cheese (such as low-moisture mozzarella, brick cheese, Monterey Jack, mild cheddar, or a mix), shredded (2 cups)

1½ cups No-Cook Marinara (page 84), Slow-Simmered Pizza Sauce (page 85), or jarred/canned pizza sauce

¼ to ½ cup finely shredded or grated parmesan or other hard, aged cheese (optional)

NOTES:

Follow the Sicilian Pan Pizza Dough recipe through step 3, let it rise until doubled, 1 to 2 hours, and then divide it in half. (You will only use one half for this recipe; put the other one in a zip-top bag, squeeze out all the air, and freeze for up to 3 months.)

Preheat the oven to 500°F with a rack in the bottom position.

Grease a (9-by-13-inch) Detroit-style pizza pan or dark metal baking pan with the olive oil. Place the dough in the pan, then press it out with your fingertips until it fills the pan all the way to the edges. If it keeps shrinking back, let the dough rest for another 15 to 20 minutes and try again. Cover with plastic wrap and let the dough rest for about 30 minutes, until it puffs up a bit and you see a few small bubbles on the surface.

Using your fingertips, press dimples all over the surface of the dough to release any large air bubbles. Arrange the pepperoni slices in a grid on the dough, then scatter on the mozzarella or other semi-firm cheese(s), making sure to get it all the way to the edges, touching the sides of the pan. (This will give your Detroit-style pizza that characteristic dark-brown caramelized crust.) Pour the pizza sauce into a spouted measuring cup and pour it in three long lines on top of the cheese. Finish with the parmesan, if using.

Bake for 15 minutes, turning once at the halfway mark, until the cheese is golden and the edges of the pizza are almost black. To double-check for doneness, use a long spatula to carefully lift the pizza from the pan; it's finished cooking when the underside of the crust is evenly browned.

Remove the pizza from the oven. Let it cool for about 5 minutes, then slide the pizza out of the pan and onto a cutting board. Cut into squares and serve.

PIZZA RULES

PHILLY-STYLE TOMATO PIE

~~~~~~

With its thick, tender crust, rich, slightly sweet tomato
sauce, and post-bake dusting of Parmigiano-Reggiano cheese,
this is the tomato pie dreams are made of. (Leave off the
cheese to keep it vegan.)

~~~~~~

MAKES 1
(13-BY-18-INCH)
PIZZA

1 recipe Sicilian Pan Pizza
Dough (page 66)

1 recipe (about 2 cups)
Slow-Simmered Pizza Sauce
(page 85)

2 tablespoons extra-virgin
olive oil, plus more for
drizzling

Kosher salt

Freshly ground black pepper

½ cup grated Parmigiano-
Reggiano cheese (optional)

Follow the Sicilian Pan Pizza Dough recipe through step 3 and let it rise for 1 to 2 hours, until it about doubles in volume.

Grease a large (13-by-18-inch) dark-colored rimmed baking sheet with the olive oil. Place the dough in the pan and gently press it out with your fingertips until it fills the pan all the way to the edges. If it keeps shrinking back, let the dough rest for another 15 to 20 minutes and try again. After the dough is pressed out all the way to the corners, cover with plastic wrap or a clean kitchen towel and let the dough rest for 45 minutes or up to 2 hours. (The longer the dough proofs, the fluffier your finished pizza crust will be.)

Preheat the oven to 500°F with a rack in the bottom position.

When the dough is finished resting in the sheet pan, dimple it with your fingertips to prevent big bubbles from forming in the oven. Then, slather on the sauce, spreading it evenly and leaving a ¼- to ½-inch border all around.

Bake for 12 to 15 minutes, rotating the baking sheet at the halfway mark, until the underside of the crust is evenly browned. (Carefully lift up the pizza with an offset or other spatula to check for doneness.)

Remove the pizza from the oven and let it cool for about 5 minutes, then use two spatulas to transfer it to a large cutting board. Season with a few pinches of salt and few grinds of black pepper, drizzle with olive oil, and dust with the grated Parmigiano-Reggiano (if using).

Cut into squares and serve warm, cold, or at room temperature.

Pizza Notes

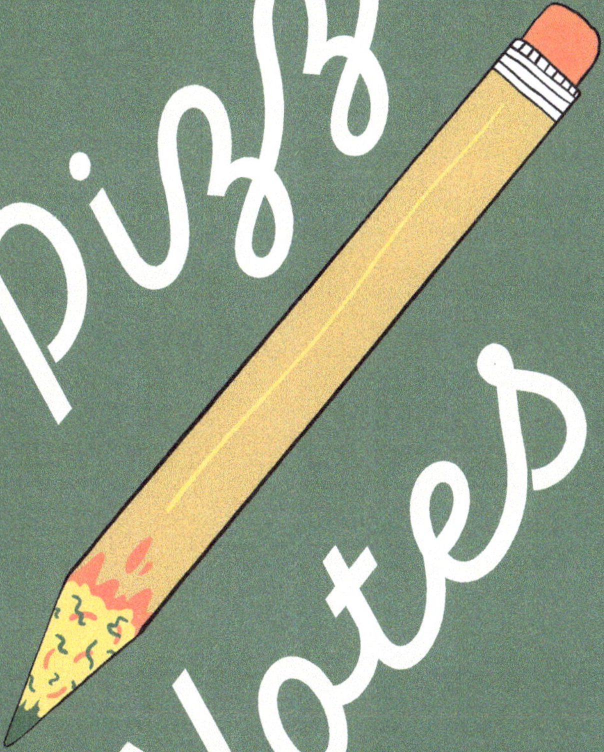

Pizza Notes

Pizza Notes

Pizza Notes

Pizza Notes ———————————————————————————

INDEX

ACKNOWLEDGMENTS

This book took a village to produce, and I'm grateful to every friend, family member, colleague, and reader who helped shepherd my idea from brainstorm to finished files.

SPECIAL THANKS TO:

JOANNA AND DANIELLE, for understanding my vision and transforming it into something way cooler than I could have imagined

JESS, for her friendship and editorial prowess

JOHN AND JACK, for never getting tired of homemade pizza

THE TNP PIZZA BRAIN TRUST, for responding to polls, sharing pizza-making woes, and weighing in on design and content ideas

THURSDAY NIGHT PIZZA READERS, whose comments and questions inspired every part of this book

. . . AND ALL THE PEOPLE WHO'VE ASKED, "Will you ever run out of pizza ideas?"—I hope, by now, you know the answer.

ABOUT THE AUTHOR

Peggy Paul Casella is a recipe developer, writer, cookbook consultant, and homemade pizza enthusiast based in Philadelphia. Her website, ThursdayNightPizza.com, hosts the largest selection of original pizza and pizza-related recipes on the Internet, and her other cookbooks include the *Teenage Mutant Ninja Turtles Pizza Cookbook* (Insight Editions, 2017) and *The Dip Deck* (Clarkson Potter, 2025).

To learn more about Peggy and her work, visit PeggyPaulCasella.com.

PeggyPaulCasella

www.ingramcontent.com/pod-product-compliance
Lightning Source LLC
Chambersburg PA
CBHW051309120626
46547CB00015B/2161